VICE

VICE

NEW AND SELECTED POEMS

Ai

W. W. NORTON & COMPANY
New York / London

These dramatic monologues are 100 percent fiction and are
merely characters created by the poet. Some of them project the
names of "real" public figures onto made-up characters in
made-up circumstances. Where the names of corporate, media,
public, or political figures are used here, those names are meant
only to denote figures, images, the stuff of imagination; they do
not denote or pretend to private information about actual
persons, living, dead, or otherwise.

For information about permission to reproduce selections from
this book, write to Permissions, W. W. Norton & Company,
Inc., 500 Fifth Avenue, New York, NY 10110.

The text of this book is composed in Bembo
with the display set in Diotima
Composition by RR Donnelley & Sons'
Allentown Digital Services Division
Manufacturing by The Haddon Craftsmen, Inc.
Book design by Judith Stagnitto Abbate / ABBATE DESIGN

Library of Congress Cataloging-in-Publication Data
Ai, 1947–
Vice : new and selected poems / Ai.
p.   cm.
Includes index.
ISBN 0-393-04705-9
I. Title.
PS3551.I2V53   1999
811'.54—dc21   98-37334
CIP

W. W. Norton & Company, Inc., 500 Fifth Avenue, New York, N.Y. 10110
http://www.wwnorton.com

W. W. Norton & Company, Ltd., 10 Coptic Street, London WC1A 1PU

3 4 5 6 7 8 9 0

VICE

NEW AND SELECTED POEMS

Ai

W. W. NORTON & COMPANY
New York / London

These dramatic monologues are 100 percent fiction and are
merely characters created by the poet. Some of them project the
names of "real" public figures onto made-up characters in
made-up circumstances. Where the names of corporate, media,
public, or political figures are used here, those names are meant
only to denote figures, images, the stuff of imagination; they do
not denote or pretend to private information about actual
persons, living, dead, or otherwise.

For information about permission to reproduce selections from
this book, write to Permissions, W. W. Norton & Company,
Inc., 500 Fifth Avenue, New York, NY 10110.

The text of this book is composed in Bembo
with the display set in Diotima
Composition by RR Donnelley & Sons'
Allentown Digital Services Division
Manufacturing by The Haddon Craftsmen, Inc.
Book design by Judith Stagnitto Abbate / ABBATE DESIGN

Library of Congress Cataloging-in-Publication Data
Ai, 1947–
Vice : new and selected poems / Ai.
p. cm.
Includes index.
ISBN 0-393-04705-9
I. Title.
PS3551.I2V53 1999
811'.54—dc21   98-37334
                            CIP

W. W. Norton & Company, Inc., 500 Fifth Avenue, New York, N.Y. 10110
http://www.wwnorton.com

W. W. Norton & Company, Ltd., 10 Coptic Street, London WC1A 1PU

3 4 5 6 7 8 9 0

THIS BOOK IS DEDICATED TO MY MOTHER.

The poems in this book have appeared in the following magazines:

The American Poetry Review: "Passing Through"; *BED OF RICE*: Momento Mori; *Caprice*: "Chance"; *Focus on Art*: "Afterschool Lessons from a Hitman," "The Paparazzi," "Star Vehicle"; *New Letters*: "Knock, Knock," "Sleeping Beauty"; *ONTHEBUS*: "Rapture," "Visitation"; *Poetry International*: "The Antihero"; *Pequod*: "Stalking Memory"; *Quarterly West*: "Back in the World"; *Rattle*: "Charisma"; *Sniper Logic*: "False Witness"

Contents

New Poems

CRUELTY

___

[1973]

TWENTY-YEAR MARRIAGE

You keep me waiting in a truck
with its one good wheel stuck in the ditch,
while you piss against the south side of a tree.
Hurry. I've got nothing on under my skirt tonight.
That still excites you, but this pickup has no windows
and the seat, one fake leather thigh,
pressed close to mine is cold.
I'm the same size, shape, make as twenty years ago,
but get inside me, start the engine;
you'll have the strength, the will to move.
I'll pull, you push, we'll tear each other in half.
Come on, baby, lay me down on my back.
Pretend you don't owe me a thing
and maybe we'll roll out of here,
leaving the past stacked up behind us;
old newspapers nobody's ever got to read again.

ABORTION

Coming home, I find you still in bed,
but when I pull back the blanket,
I see your stomach is flat as an iron.
You've done it, as you warned me you would
and left the fetus wrapped in wax paper
for me to look at. My son.
Woman, loving you no matter what you do,
what can I say, except that I've heard
the poor have no children, just small people
and there is room only for one man in this house.

THE COUNTRY MIDWIFE: A DAY

I bend over the woman.
This is the third time between abortions.
I dip a towel into a bucket of hot water
and catch the first bit of blood,
as the blue-pink dome of a head breaks through.
A scraggy, red child comes out of her into my hands
like warehouse ice sliding down the chute.

It's done, the stink of birth, Old Grizzly
rears up on his hind legs in front of me
and I want to go outside,
but the air smells the same there too.
The woman's left eye twitches
and beneath her, a stain as orange as sunrise
spreads over the sheet.
I lift my short, blunt fingers to my face
and I let her bleed, Lord, I let her bleed.

CRUELTY

The hoof-marks on the dead wildcat
gleam in the dark.
You are naked, as you drag it up on the porch.
That won't work either.
Drinking ice water hasn't,
nor having the bedsprings snap fingers
to help us keep rhythm.
I've never once felt anything
that might get close. Can't you see?
The thing I want most is hard,
running toward my own teeth
and it bites back.

THE TENANT FARMER

Hailstones puncture the ground,
as I sit at the table, rubbing a fork.
My woman slides a knife across her lips,
then lays it beside a cup of water.
Each day she bites another notch in her thumb
and I pretend relief is coming
as the smooth black tire, Earth,
wheels around the sun without its patch of topsoil
and my mouth speaks: *wheat, barley, red cabbage,*
roll on home to Jesus,
it's too late now you're dead.

WHY CAN'T I LEAVE YOU?

You stand behind the old black mare,
dressed as always in that red shirt,
stained from sweat, the crying of the armpits,
that will not stop for anything,
stroking her rump, while the barley goes unplanted.
I pick up my suitcase and set it down,
as I try to leave you again.
I smooth the hair back from your forehead.
I think with your laziness and the drought too,
you'll be needing my help more than ever.
You take my hands, I nod
and go to the house to unpack,
having found another reason to stay.

I undress, then put on my white lace slip
for you to take off, because you like that
and when you come in, you pull down the straps
and I unbutton your shirt.
I know we can't give each other any more
or any less than what we have.
There is safety in that, so much
that I can never get past the packing,
the begging you to please, if I can't make you happy,
come close between my thighs
and let me laugh for you from my second mouth.

I HAVE GOT TO STOP LOVING YOU
SO I HAVE KILLED MY BLACK GOAT

His kidney floats in a bowl,
a beige, flat fish, around whom parasites, slices of lemon,
break through the surface of hot broth, then sink below,
as I bend, face down in the steam, breathing in.
I hear this will cure anything.

When I am finished, I walk up to him.
He hangs from a short wooden post,
tongue stuck out of his mouth,
tasting the hay-flavored air.
A bib of flies gather at his throat
and further down, where he is open
and bare of all his organs,
I put my hand in, stroke him once,
then taking it out, look at the sky.
The stormclouds there break open
and raindrops, yellow as black cats' eyes, come down
each a tiny river, hateful and alone.

Wishing I could get out of this alive, I hug myself.
It is hard to remember if he suffered much.

YOUNG FARM WOMAN ALONE

What could I do with a man?—
pull him on like these oxhide boots,
the color of plums, dipped in blue ink
and stomp hell out of my loneliness,
this hoe that with each use grows sharper.

ONE MAN DOWN

Your brother brings you home from hunting,
slung over your horse, dead,
with the wild boar tied down beside you.
I ask no questions.

He throws the boar at my feet,
hands me the red licorice he promised.
I drop my shawl
and his hands cover my breasts.
He whispers of a dress in town,
while I unbutton my skirt.

I sit on the ground, waiting,
while he loosens his belt.
He smiles, swings it across my face,
then pushes me back. I keep my eyes open.
The hound's paws bloody the tiles
lining the flower bed.
The bitch walks behind him, licking his tracks.
I scratch the flesh above me.
The odor of fresh meat
digs a finger in my nostrils.
The horse rears,
your body slides from the black saddle
like a bedroll of fine velvet.
I laugh, close my eyes, and relax.

HANGMAN

In the fields, the silos open their mouths
and let the grain dribble down their sides,
for they are overflowing.
The farmers swing their scythes, brows dripping blood.
They have had the passion ripped out of their chests
and share no brotherhood with the wheat,

while far across the open land,
the Hangman mounts an empty scaffold.
He slides his hands over the coarse-grained cedar
and smells the whole Lebanese coast
in the upraised arms of Kansas.
The rope's stiff bristles prick his fingers,
as he holds it and lifts himself above the trap door.

He touches the wood again.
This will be his last hanging
and anyway he has seen other fields,
workmen nailing brass spikes into the scaffolds
and rope which coiled and uncoiled
in the laps of farm women.
He places his foot on the step going down
and nearby, a scarecrow explodes,
sending tiny slivers of straw into his eyes.

THE SWEET

The man steps in out of the blizzard with his Klootch,
his Eskimo prostitute and the room heats up, as they
cross the floor. I know he is dying and I spin a half
dollar around on the bar, then slide my eyes over the woman.
She has a seal's body. Her face is a violet in the center
of the moon. The half dollar falls over, I remind myself
that to love a Klootch is always to be filled with emptiness,
turn and lift my glass.

I shake my head, drink. When I hear retreating footsteps,
I turn. The man stands at the door, facing me. His hand
gropes out, as the woman backs off and I see the Northern
Lights flare up in his eyes, before he stumbles and falls.
The woman leans back against the wall. I pick up the half
dollar, spin it around again and go to her. We walk out
into the darkness and I am cold as I squeeze her buttocks,
her blue, dwarf stars.

THE HITCHHIKER

The Arizona wind dries out my nostrils
and the heat of the sidewalk burns my shoes,
as a woman drives up slowly.
I get in, grinning at a face I do not like,
but I slide my arm across the top of the seat
and rest it lightly against her shoulder.
We turn off into the desert,
then I reach inside my pocket and touch the switchblade.

We stop, and as she moves closer to me, my hands ache,
but somehow, I get the blade into her chest.
I think a song: "Everybody needs somebody,
everybody needs somebody to love,"
as the black numerals 35 roll out of her right eye
inside one small tear.
Laughing, I snap my fingers. Rape, murder, I got you
in the sight of my gun.

I move off toward the street.
My feet press down in it,
familiar with the hot, soft asphalt
that caresses them.
The sun slips down into its cradle behind the mountains
and it is hot, hotter than ever
and I like it.

CUBA, 1962

When the rooster jumps up on the windowsill
and spreads his red-gold wings,
I wake, thinking it is the sun
and call Juanita, hearing her answer,
but only in my mind.
I know she is already outside,
breaking the cane off at ground level,
using only her big hands.
I get the machete and walk among the cane,
until I see her, lying face-down in the dirt.

Juanita, dead in the morning like this.
I raise the machete—
what I take from the earth, I give back—
and cut off her feet.
I lift the body and carry it to the wagon,
where I load the cane to sell in the village.
Whoever tastes my woman in his candy, his cake,
tastes something sweeter than this sugar cane;
it is grief.
If you eat too much of it, you want more,
you can never get enough.

CHILD BEATER

Outside, the rain, pinafore of gray water, dresses the town
and I stroke the leather belt,
as she sits in the rocking chair,
holding a crushed paper cup to her lips.
I yell at her, but she keeps rocking;
back, her eyes open, forward, they close.
Her body, somehow fat, though I feed her only once a day,
reminds me of my own just after she was born.
It's been seven years, but I still can't forget how I felt.
How heavy it feels to look at her.

I lay the belt on a chair
and get her dinner bowl.
I hit the spoon against it, set it down
and watch her crawl to it,
pausing after each forward thrust of her legs
and when she takes her first bite,
I grab the belt and beat her across the back
until her tears, beads of salt-filled glass, falling,
shatter on the floor.

I move off. I let her eat,
while I get my dog's chain leash from the closet.
I whirl it around my head.
O daughter, so far, you've only had a taste of icing,
are you ready now for some cake?

EVERYTHING: ELOY, ARIZONA, 1956

Tin shack, where my baby sleeps on his back
the way the hound taught him;
highway, black zebra, with one white stripe;
nickel in my pocket for chewing gum;
you think you're all I've got.
But when the 2 ton rolls to a stop
and the driver gets out,
I sit down in the shade and wave each finger,
saving my whole hand till the last.
He's keys, tires, a fire lit in his belly
in the diner up the road.
I'm red toenails, tight blue halter, black slip.
He's mine tonight. I don't know him.
He can only hurt me a piece at a time.

KILLING FLOOR

[1979]

KILLING FLOOR

1. RUSSIA, 1927

On the day the sienna-skinned man
held my shoulders between his spade-shaped hands,
easing me down into the azure water of Jordan,
I woke ninety-three million miles from myself,
Lev Davidovich Bronstein,
shoulder-deep in the Volga,
while the cheap dye of my black silk shirt darkened the water.

My head wet, water caught in my lashes.
Am I blind?
I rub my eyes, then wade back to shore,
undress and lie down,
until Stalin comes from his place beneath the birch tree.
He folds my clothes
and I button myself in my marmot coat,
and together we start the long walk back to Moscow.
He doesn't ask, *what did you see in the river?*,
but I hear the hosts of a man drowning in water and holiness,
the castrati voices I can't recognize,
skating on knives, from trees, from air
on the thin ice of my last night in Russia.
Leon Trotsky. Bread.
I want to scream, but silence holds my tongue
with small spade-shaped hands
and only this comes, so quietly

Stalin has to press his ear to my mouth:
I have only myself. Put me on the train.
I won't look back.

2. MEXICO, 1940

At noon today, I woke from a nightmare:
my friend Jacques ran toward me with an ax,
as I stepped from the train in Alma-Ata.
He was dressed in yellow satin pants and shirt.
A marigold in winter.
When I held out my arms to embrace him,
he raised the ax and struck me at the neck,
my head fell to one side, hanging only by skin.
A river of sighs poured from the cut.

3. MEXICO, AUGUST 20, 1940

The machine-gun bullets
hit my wife in the legs,
then zigzagged up her body.
I took the shears, cut open her gown
and lay on top of her for hours.
Blood soaked through my clothes
and when I tried to rise, I couldn't.

I wake then. Another nightmare.
I rise from my desk, walk to the bedroom
and sit down at my wife's mirrored vanity.
I rouge my cheeks and lips,
stare at my bone-white, speckled egg of a face:
lined and empty.
I lean forward and see Jacques's reflection.
I half-turn, smile, then turn back to the mirror.

He moves from the doorway,
lifts the pickax
and strikes the top of my head.
My brain splits.
The pickax keeps going
and when it hits the tile floor,
it flies from his hands,
a black dove on whose back I ride,
two men, one cursing,
the other blessing all things:
Lev Davidovich Bronstein,
I step from Jordan without you.

NOTHING BUT COLOR

for Yukio Mishima

I didn't write Etsuko,
I sliced her open.
She was carmine inside
like a sea bass
and empty.
No viscera, nothing but color.
I love you like that, boy.
I pull the kimono down around your shoulders
and kiss you.
Then you let it fall open.
Each time, I cut you a little
and when you leave, I take the piece,
broil it, dip it in ginger sauce
and eat it. It burns my mouth so.
You laugh, holding me belly-down
with your body.
So much hurting to get to this moment,
when I'm beneath you,
wanting it to go on and to end.

At midnight, you say *see you tonight*
and I answer *there won't be any tonight,*
but you just smile, swing your sweater
over your head and tie the sleeves around your neck.
I hear you whistling long after you disappear
down the subway steps,
as I walk back home, my whole body tingling.

I undress
and put the bronze sword on my desk
beside the crumpled sheet of rice paper.
I smooth it open
and read its single sentence:
I meant to do it.
No. It should be common and feminine
like *I can't go on sharing him,*
or something to imply that.
Or the truth:
that I saw in myself
the five signs of the decay of the angel
and you were holding on, watching and free,
that I decided to go out
with the pungent odor
of this cold and consuming passion in my nose: death.
Now, I've said it. That vulgar word
that drags us down to the worms, sightless, predestined.
Goddamn you, boy.
Nothing I said mattered to you;
that bullshit about Etsuko or about killing myself.
I tear the note, then burn it.
The alarm clock goes off. 5:45 A.M.
I take the sword and walk into the garden.
I look up. The sun, the moon,
two round teeth rock together
and the light of one chews up the other.
I stab myself in the belly,
wait, then stab myself again. Again.
It's snowing. I'll turn to ice,
but I'll burn anyone who touches me.
I start pulling my guts out,

those red silk cords,
spiraling skyward,
and I'm climbing them
past the moon and the sun,
past darkness
into white.
I mean to live.

TALKING TO HIS REFLECTION IN
A SHALLOW POND

for Yasunari Kawabata

Chrysanthemum and nightshade:
I live on them,
though air is what I need.
I wish I could breath like you,
asleep, or even awake,
just resting your head
on the pillow wrapped in black crepe
that I brought you from Sweden.
I hoped you'd die,
your mouth open, lips dry and split,
and red like pomegranate seeds.
But now, I only want you to suffer.
I drop a stone in the pond
and it sinks through you.
Japan isn't sliding into the Pacific
this cool April morning, you are.
Yasunari Kawabata, I'm talking to you;
just drop like that stone
through your own reflection.
You stretch your lean hands toward me
and I take them.
Water covers my face, my whole head,
as I inhale myself:
cold, very cold.
Suddenly, I pull back.
For a while, I watch you struggle,

then I start walking back to my studio.
But something is wrong.
There's water everywhere
and you're standing above me.
I stare up at you from the still, clear water.
You open your mouth and I open mine.
We both speak slowly.
Brother, you deserve to suffer,
You deserve the best:
this moment, death without end.

29 (A DREAM IN TWO PARTS)

1.

Night, that old woman, jabs the sun
with a pitchfork,
and dyes the cheesecloth sky blue-violet,
as I sit at the kitchen table,
bending small pieces of wire in hoops.
You come in naked.
No. Do it yourself.

2.

I'm a nine-year-old girl,
skipping beside a single hoop of daylight.
I hear your voice.
I start running. You lift me in your arms.
I holler. The little girl turns.
Her hoop rolls out of sight.
Something warm seeps through my gown onto my belly.
She never looks back.

SHE DIDN'T EVEN WAVE

for Marilyn Monroe

I buried Mama in her wedding dress
and put gloves on her hands,
but I couldn't do much about her face,
blue-black and swollen,
so I covered it with a silk scarf.
I hike my dress up to my thighs
and rub them,
watching you tip the mortuary fan back and forth.
Hey. Come on over. Cover me all up
like I was never here. Just never.
Come on. I don't know why I talk like that.
It was a real nice funeral. Mama's.
I touch the rhinestone heart pinned to my blouse.
Honey, let's look at it again.
See. It's bright like the lightning that struck her.

I walk outside
and face the empty house.
You put your arms around me. Don't.
Let me wave goodbye.
Mama never got a chance to do it.
She was walking toward the barn
when it struck her. I didn't move;
I just stood at the screen door.
Her whole body was light.
I'd never seen anything so beautiful.
I remember how she cried in the kitchen

a few minutes before.
She said, *God. Married.*
I don't believe it, Jean, I won't.
He takes and takes and you just give.   .
At the door, she held out her arms
and I ran to her.
She squeezed me so tight:
I was all short of breath.
And she said, *don't do it.*
In ten years, your heart will be eaten out
and you'll forgive him, or some other man, even that
and it will kill you.
Then she walked outside.
And I kept saying, I've got to, Mama,
hug me again. Please don't go.

ICE

breaks up in obelisks on the river,
as I stand beside your grave.
I tip my head back.
Above me, the same sky you loved,
that shawl of cotton wool,
frozen around the shoulders of Minnesota.
I'm cold and so far from Texas
and my father, who gave me to you.
I was twelve, a Choctaw, a burden.
A woman, my father said, raising my skirt.
Then he showed you the roll of green gingham,
stained red, that I'd tried to crush to powder
with my small hands. I close my eyes,

and it is March 1866 again.
I'm fourteen, wearing a white smock.
I straddle the rocking horse you made for me
and stroke the black mane cut from my own hair.
Sunrise hugs you from behind,
as you walk through the open door
and lay the velvet beside me.
I give you the ebony box
with the baby's skull inside
and you set it on your work table,
comb your pale blond hair with one hand,
then nail it shut.
When the new baby starts crying, I cover my ears,

watching as you lift him from the cradle
and lay him on the pony-skin rug.
I untie the red scarf, knotted at my throat,
climb off the horse and bend over you.
I slip the scarf around your neck,
and pull it tight, remembering:
I strangled the other baby,
laid her on your stomach while you were asleep.
You break my hold and pull me to the floor.
I scratch you, bite your lips, your face,
then you cry out,
and I open and close my hands
around a row of bear teeth.

I open my eyes.
I wanted you then and now,
and I never let you know.
I kiss the headstone.
Tonight, wake me like always.
Talk and I'll listen,
while you lie on the pallet
resting your arms behind your head,
telling me about the wild rice in the marshes
and the empty .45 you call *Grace of God* that keeps you alive,
as we slide forward, without bitterness, decade by decade,
becoming transparent. Everlasting.

THE RAVINE

I wake, sweating, reach for your rosary and drop it.
I roll over on the straw and sit up. It's light out.
I pull on my pants, slip into my rope sandals
and go outside, where you sit
against a sack of beans.
I touch the chicken feathers
stuck to the purple splotches of salve on your stomach.
Your eyes, two tiny bowls of tar
set deep in your skull, stare straight ahead
and your skin is almost the color of your eyes,
because Death pressed his black face against yours.
I put our daughter in your lap,
lift you both and walk to the ravine's edge.
I step over—

—the years fly up in my face like a fine gray dust.
I'm twenty. I buy you with matches, a mirror and a rifle.
You don't talk. While I ride the mule downhill,
you walk beside me in a blue cotton dress.
Your flat Indian face shines with boar grease.
Your wide feet sink deep in the spring mud.
You raise your hands to shade your eyes
from the sudden explosion of sunlight
through the umber clouds.
In that brightness, you separate into five stained-glass women.
Four of you are floating north, south, east and west.
I reach out, shatter you in each direction.

I start to fall, catch myself,
get off the mule and make you ride.
You cry silently, ashamed to let me walk.
At bottom, you look back.
I keep going. Up a few yards,
I strip two thin pieces of bark off a tamarisk tree,
and we chew on them, sweetening the only way home.

THE KID

My sister rubs the doll's face in mud,
then climbs through the truck window.
She ignores me as I walk around it,
hitting the flat tires with an iron rod.
The old man yells for me to help hitch the team,
but I keep walking around the truck, hitting harder,
until my mother calls.
I pick up a rock and throw it at the kitchen window,
but it falls short.
The old man's voice bounces off the air like a ball
I can't lift my leg over.

I stand beside him, waiting, but he doesn't look up
and I squeeze the rod, raise it, his skull splits open.
Mother runs toward us. I stand still,
get her across the spine as she bends over him.
I drop the rod and take the rifle from the house.
Roses are red, violets are blue,
one bullet for the black horse, two for the brown.
They're down quick. I spit, my tongue's bloody;
I've bitten it. I laugh, remember the one out back.
I catch her climbing from the truck, shoot.
The doll lands on the ground with her.
I pick it up, rock it in my arms.
Yeah. I'm Jack, Hogarth's son.
I'm nimble, I'm quick.
In the house, I put on the old man's best suit

and his patent leather shoes.
I pack my mother's satin nightgown
and my sister's doll in the suitcase.
Then I go outside and cross the fields to the highway.
I'm fourteen. I'm a wind from nowhere.
I can break your heart.

I CAN'T GET STARTED

for Ira Hayes

1. SATURDAY NIGHT

A coyote eats chunks of the moon,
the night hen's yellow egg,
while I lie drunk, in a ditch.
Suddenly, a huge combat boot
punches a hole through the sky
and falls toward me.
I wave my arms. Get back.
It keeps coming.

2. SUNDAY MORNING

I stumble out of the ditch
and make it to the shack.
I shoot a few holes in the roof,
then stare at the paper clippings of Iwo Jima.
I remember raising that rag
of red, white and blue,
afraid that if I let go, I'd live.
The bullets never touched me.
Nothing touches me.

Around noon, I make a cup of coffee
and pour a teaspoon of pepper in it
to put the fire out.
I hum between sips
and when I finish, I hug myself.
I'm burning from the bottom up,

a bottle of flesh,
kicked across the hardwood years.
I pass gin and excuses from hand to mouth,
but it's me. It's me.
I'm the one dirty habit
I just can't break.

PENTECOST

for Myself

Rosebud Morales, my friend,
before you deserted,
you'd say anyone can kill an Indian
and forget it the same instant,
that it will happen to me, Emiliano Zapata.
But my men want more corn for tortillas,
more pigs, more chickens, more chilis
and land.
If I haven't got a gun or a knife,
I'll fight with a pitchfork or a hoe,
to take them from the bosses,
those high-flying birds,
with the pomade glistening on their hair,
as they promenade into their coffins.
And if I'm killed, if we're all killed right now,
we'll go on, the true Annunciation.

Rosebud, how beautiful this day is.
I'm riding to meet Guajardo.
He'll fight with me now,
against Carranza.
When I get to the hacienda, it's quiet.
Not many soldiers,
a sorrel horse, its reins held
by a woman in a thin, white American dress
and Guajardo standing on a balcony.
I get off my horse and start up the steps.

My legs burn, my chest,
my jaw, my head.
There's a hill in front of me;
it's slippery, I have to use my hands to climb it.
At the top, it's raining fire and blood
on rows and rows of black corn.
Machetes are scattered everywhere.
I grab one and start cutting the stalks.
When they hit the ground,
they turn into men.
I yell at them.
You're damned in the cradle,
in the grave, even in Heaven.
Dying doesn't end anything.
Get up. Swing those machetes.
You can't steal a man's glory
without a goddamned fight.
Boys, take the land, take it; it's yours.
If you suffer in the grave,
You can kill from it.

THE GILDED MAN

In 1561, on an expedition down the Marañon and Amazon to find El Dorado, Lope de Aguirre killed Urzúa, the leader of the expedition, then scores of others. He declared rebellion against Spain and set out to conquer Peru, con el alma en los dientes, *with his soul between his teeth.*

1. THE ORINOCO, 1561

For a while today, the rafts almost float side by side.
The river is as smooth and soft
as the strip of emerald velvet
sewn around the hem of your dress, my daughter.
I call you Vera Cruz,
because you are the true cross
from which I hang by ropes of gold.
The word *father,* a spear of dark brown hair,
enters my side and disintegrates,
leaving me whole again,
smelling of quinces and gunpowder
and your stale, innocent breath.
What is it?
you whisper. I take your hand
and we walk into the jungle.
I watch you raise your dress, bend,
then tear your petticoat with your teeth.
You fold the torn cloth
and slide it between your legs.
Then you hold out your bloody hands
and I wipe them on my shirt,
already red from fighting.
Urzúa is dead. Guzmán is dead. There is no Spain.

I'm hunting El Dorado, the Gilded Man.
When I catch him. I'll cut him up.
I'll start with his feet
and give them to you to wear as earrings.
Talk to me.
I hear nothing but the monkeys squealing above me.
I point my arquebus at a silhouette in the trees, and fire.
For a moment, I think it's you falling toward me,
your dress shredding to sepia light.
I drop the arquebus and stretch out my hands.
Fall, darling, fall into me.
Lope de Aguirre. I hear my name
as I lift you in my arms.
Daughter. Beautiful.
You weigh no more than ashes.

2. BARQUISIMETO, VENEZUELA, OCTOBER 27, 1561

Today it rained vengefully and hard
and my men deserted me.
My kingdom was as close
as calling it by name. Peru.
I braid your hair, daughter,
as you kneel with your head in my lap.
I talk softly, stopping to press your face to my chest.
Vera Cruz. Listen. My heart is speaking.
I am the fishes, the five loaves.
The women, the men I killed simply ate me.
There is no dying, only living in death.
I was their salvation.
I am absolved by their hunger.
El Dorado, the kingdom of gold,

is only a tapestry I wove from their blood.
Stand up. My enemies will kill me
and they won't be merciful with you.
I unsheathe my dagger. Your mouth opens.
I can't hear you. I want to. Tell me you love me.
You cover your mouth with your hands.
I stab you, then fall beside your body.
Vera Cruz. See my skin covered with gold dust
and tongues of flame,
transfigured by the pentecost of my own despair.
I, Aguirre the wanderer, Aguirre the traitor,
the Gilded Man.
Does God think that because it rains in torrents
I am not to go to Peru and destroy the world?
God. The boot heel an inch above your head is mine.
God, say your prayers.

SIN

[1986]

TWO BROTHERS

A Fiction

1

Night tightens its noose.
You swim toward me out of sleep
like an eel,
as I put the glass canister
beside you on the bed.
Death, Bobby, hit me
like the flat of a hand.
Imagine you are made of crystal
and someone ice picks you
and you shatter,
all your cells coming
almost to despair
it is so good. Dallas. Dallas.
I turn toward the window,
then turn back to you.
Remember that Crayola drawing
of John-John's?—
the black smoke coming out the roof
of the White House
like curly black hair.
How Jackie spanked his hand
and drew him another
with angels lifting up?
Our own childhoods?—
days of ease and grace.
The good life sucking us deeper

and deeper in
toward its hot, liquid center,
where seasoned with the right diction,
schools, and politics
we would fry crisp and greaseless.
King for a day,
that's who I was.
I drove power,
the solid-gold Cadillac.
Go ahead, frown.
Tell me about the sin of pride
and I'll tell you
about the lie of forgiveness.
It wasn't Oswald killed me,
it was envy.

2

"I have this dream, Jack," you say.
"I'm at Arlington. It's twilight.
Thousands of funeral markers
rise from the ground
like dirty alabaster arms.
It's here, pilgrim,
they seem to say.
And then I'm in a room.
A man is counting green bills
sharp enough to cut,
while I pry the lid off a barrel
and peer down into it,
as if inside, there are dark green pickles
or steel-blue fish,
as if I were a boy

on a crowded street in Russia
with my hand around a coin
and the other in my brother's hand.
And while I scuff my shoe
and try to decide,
from far away I hear bugles, hoofbeats,
I see my brother's head
suddenly rise from his body
like a tiny pink ball
on a spout of dark red water,
clear past the rooftops
into the serene evening sky.
I am that boy, Jack,
dipping his hands
in the one standing barrel,
into water warm as blood,
with nothing to say to anybody,
except, 'My brother is the moon.' "

3

Riddles, I say,
lifting the lid off the canister.
I pull out a wet, gray mass,
stare at it, then put it back.
Some African tribes
eat the brains of their dead.
It brings them closer;
it kills them too.
But whatever it takes, Bobby, right?
I look out the window
at the deep rose welts of dawn,
streaking the sky's broad back,

then hand you the canister.
You lift out my brain.
When you bite down, I burn.
The air smells like creosote
and I stand before you,
my skin plump and pink,
my wounds healed.
I put my arms around you
and you disappear into me . . .

I stare at myself in the mirror:
Jack Kennedy,
thinner now, almost ascetic,
wearing the exhaust fumes of L.A.
like a sharkskin suit,
while the quarter moon
hangs from heaven,
a swing on a gold chain. My throne.
I step back and knot my tie.
Bobby, it's all a matter of showmanship.
You have to have the ability to entertain,
to stand like P. T. Barnum
in the enchanted center
of the public eye,
to drop your pants now and then
and have the crowd
cry for more,
to give it to them,
to take those encores,
till like the clown in Piaf's song
the show is all there is,
and the bravos, the bravos.

You give the people what they want, Bobby,
someone they can't help loving
like a father or an uncle,
someone who through his own magical fall
lifts them above the slime
of their daily lives.
Not God made man,
but man made God.
I step back to the mirror.
Break a leg, kid, I say to myself.
Give 'em a miracle.
Give 'em Hollywood.
Give 'em Saint Jack.

BLUE SUEDE SHOES

A Fiction

1

Heliotrope sprouts from your shoes, brother,
their purplish color going Chianti
at the beginning of evening,
while you sit on the concrete step.
You curse, stand up, and come toward me.
In the lamplight, I see your eyes,
the zigzags of bright red in them.
"Bill's shot up," you say.
"Remember how he walked
on the balls of his feet like a dancer,
him, a boxer and so graceful
in his blue suede shoes?
Jesus, he could stayed home, Joe,
he coulda had the world by the guts,
but he gets gunned,
he gets strips of paper
tumbling out of his pockets like confetti."

Is Bea here? I say
and start for the house.
"No," you say. "This splits us, Joe.
You got money, education, friends.
You understand. I'm talking about family
and you ain't it.
The dock is my brother."
Lou, I say and step closer,

once I was fifteen, celestial.
Mom and Pop called me sweetheart
and I played the piano in the parlor
on Sunday afternoons.
There was ice cream.
Your girl wore a braid down the center of her back.
The sun had a face and it was mine.
You loved me, you sonofabitch, everybody did.
In 1923, you could count the golden boys on your fingers
and I was one of them. Me, Joe McCarthy.
I gave up music for Justice,
divorce, and small-time litigation.
And you moved here to Cleveland—
baseball, hard work, beer halls,
days fishing Lake Erie,
more money than a man like you
could ever earn on a farm
and still not enough.
Pop died in bed in his own house
because of my money.
Share, he always said, *you share*
what you have with your family
or you're nothing. You got nobody, boys.
Will you cut me off now
like you did
when I could have helped my nephew,
when you hated the way he hung on to me,
the way he listened when I talked
like I was a wise man? Wasn't I?
I could already see a faint red haze
on the horizon;
a diamond-headed hammer

slamming down on the White House;
a sickle cutting through the legs
of every man, woman, and child in America.
You know what people tell me today,
they say, *You whistle the tune, Joe,
and we'll dance.*
But my own brother sits it out.

2

A man gets bitter, Lou,
he gets so bitter
he could vomit himself up.
It happened to Bill.
He wasn't young anymore.
He knew he'd had it
that night last July
lying on a canvas of his own blood.
After a few months, he ran numbers
and he was good at it, but he was scared.
His last pickup
he stood outside the colored church
and heard voices
and he started to shake.
He thought he'd come all apart,
that he couldn't muscle it anymore,
and he skimmed cream for the first time—
$10s, $20s.

You say you would have died in his place,
but I don't believe it.
You couldn't give up your whore on Thursdays
and Bea the other nights of the week,

the little extra that comes in off the dock.
You know what I mean.
The boys start ticking—
they put their hands in the right place
and the mouse runs down the clock.
It makes you hot,
but I just itch
and when I itch, I want to smash something.
I want to condemn and condemn,
to see people squirm,
but other times,
I just go off in a dream—
I hear the Mills Brothers
singing in the background,
Up a lazy river,
then the fog clears
and I'm standing at Stalin's grave
and he's lying in an open box.
I get down on top of him
and stomp him,
till I puncture him
and this stink rises up.
I nearly black out,
but I keep stomping,
till I can smell fried trout, coffee.
And Truman's standing up above me
with his hand out
and I wake up always with the same thought:
the Reds are my enemies.
Every time I'm sitting at that big table in D.C.
and so-and-so's taking the Fifth,
or crying, or naming names,

I'm stomping his soul.
I can look inside you, Lou,
just like I do those sonsofbitches.
You got a hammer up your ass,
a sickle in between your percale sheets?
Threaten me, you red-hearted bastard. Come on.
I'll bring you to heel.

3

Yesterday Bill comes by the hotel
and he sits on the bed, but he can't relax.
Uncle, he says, and points at his feet,
all I ever wanted was this pair of blue suede shoes,
and he takes out a pawn ticket,
turns it over in his hand, then he gets up,
and at the door holds it out to me
and says, *You keep it.*

Today I go down to the pawnshop
and this is what I get back—a .38.
Bill didn't even protect himself.
You have to understand what happened to him,
in a country like this,
the chances he had.

Remember Dorothy and the Yellow Brick Road?
There's no pot of gold at the end,
but we keep walking that road,
red-white-and-blue ears of corn
steaming in our minds: America,
the only thing between us
and the Red Tide.

But some of us are straw—
we burn up like Bill in the dawn's early light.
He didn't deserve to live.
This morning, when I heard he was dead,
I didn't feel anything.
I stood looking out the window at the lake
and I thought for a moment
the whole Seventh Fleet was sailing away beneath me,
flags waving, men on deck,
shining like bars of gold,
and there, on the bow of the last ship,
Dorothy stood waving up at me.
As she passed slowly under my window,
I spit on her.
She just stared at me,
as if she didn't understand.
But she did.
She gave up the Emerald City
for a memory.
I'd never do that, never.
I'm an American.
I shall not want.
There's nothing that doesn't belong to me.

THE PRISONER

1

Yesterday, the man who calls himself "Our Father"
made me crawl on smashed Coke bottles.
Today, I sleep. I think I sleep,
till someone beats on the door, with what?—
sticks, pans—but I don't move.
I'm used to it.
Still, when Our Father rushes into the room
and drags me out, I feel the old fear.
In the interrogation room,
he knocks me to the floor,
then sits on the side of his desk,
his arms folded, that sad look on his face
I know so well. He shakes his head slowly,
stops, and smiles.
"I've got something special today," he says,
"for a fucking whore of a terrorist bitch."
I want to say nothing,
knowing how denial angers him,
but I can't stop myself.
I'm not a terrorist, I say.
"That's not what I heard," he replies, standing up.
"Aren't you the friend of a friend of a friend
of a terrorist sonofabitch
who was heard two years ago to say
that someone ought to do something
about this government?"

I don't answer.
Already, I've begun to admit that it must be true.
"I lack just one thing," he says, "the name."
"I know you think you're innocent,
but you aren't.
Everyone is guilty."
He slaps me, then pushes one side of my face
toward the green glass.

2

I've been stung by a swarm of bees.
I'm eight. I'm running for the pond
on my uncle Oscar's farm.
Oscar, I cry. Our Father sighs deeply,
lifts me up, and sets me down in a chair.
"This Oscar," he says, handing me a notebook and pen,
"where can I find him?"
I don't hesitate, as I take the pen
and set it down
on the clean, blank paper.

3

Our Father lets me off
a block from my apartment.
He keeps the motor running,
but comes and leans
against the car beside me.
I try to guess the month. March, April? I say.
He tells me it's September,
to just take a look at the sky.
Then he tells me he was a prisoner once too.
I stare at his face,

the dry, sallow skin,
the long scar running from temple to chin.
"Oh this," he touches the scar gently,
"I got this playing soccer.
No, the real scars don't show.
You should know that.
You need time, though, to sort it all out.
I'm still a young man,
but sometimes I feel as old as the Bible.
But this is a celebration."
He takes a bottle of wine from the car
and we drink, while the stars glitter above us.
Done, he tosses the bottle into the street.
"Freedom," he says, "freedom is something you earn.
The others don't understand that, but we do."

CONVERSATION

for Robert Lowell

We smile at each other
and I lean back against the wicker couch.
How does it feel to be dead? I say.
You touch my knees with your blue fingers.
And when you open your mouth,
a ball of yellow light falls to the floor
and burns a hole through it.
Don't tell me, I say. I don't want to hear.
Did you ever, you start,
wear a certain kind of silk dress
and just by accident,
so inconsequential you barely notice it,
your fingers graze that dress
and you hear the sound of a knife cutting paper,
you see it too
and you realize how that image
is simply the extension of another image,
that your own life
is a chain of words
that one day will snap.
Words, you say, young girls in a circle, holding hands,
and beginning to rise heavenward
in their confirmation dresses,
like white helium balloons,
the wreaths of flowers on their heads spinning,

and above all that,
that's where I'm floating,
and that's what it's like
only ten times clearer,
ten times more horrible.
Could anyone alive survive it?

MORE

for James Wright

Last night, I dreamed of America.
It was prom night.
She lay down under the spinning globes
at the makeshift bandstand
in her worn-out dress
and too-high heels,
the gardenia
pinned at her waist
was brown and crumbling into itself.
What's it worth, she cried,
this land of Pilgrims' pride?
As much as love, I answered. More.
The globes spun.
I never won anything, I said,
I lost time and lovers, years,
but you, purple mountains,
you amber waves of grain, belong to me
as much as I do to you.
She sighed,
the band played,
the skin fell away from her bones.
Then the room went black
and I woke.
I want my life back,
the days of too much clarity,
the nights smelling of rage,
but it's gone.

If I could shift my body
that is too weak now,
I'd lie face down on this hospital bed,
this icy water called Ohio River.
I'd float past all the sad towns,
past all the dreamers onshore
with their hands out.
I'd hold on, I'd hold,
till the weight,
till the awful heaviness
tore from me,
sank to bottom and stayed.
Then I'd stand up
like Lazarus
and walk home across the water.

THE GOOD SHEPHERD:
ATLANTA, 1981

I lift the boy's body
from the trunk,
set it down,
then push it over the embankment
with my foot.
I watch it roll
down into the river
and feel I'm rolling with it,
feel the first cold slap of the water,
wheeze and fall down on one knee.
So tired, so cold.
Lord, I need a new coat,
not polyester, but wool,
new and pure
like the little lamb
I killed tonight.
With my right hand,
that same hand that hits
with such force,
I push myself up gently.
I know what I'd like—
some hot cocoa by the heater.

Once home, I stand at the kitchen sink,
letting the water run
till it overflows the pot,

then I remember the blood
in the bathroom
and so upstairs.
I take cleanser,
begin to scrub
the tub, tiles, the toilet bowl,
then the bathroom.
Mop, vacuum, and dust rag.
Work, work for the joy of it,
for the black boys
who know too much,
but not enough to stay away,
and sometimes a girl, the girls too.
How their hands
grab at my ankles, my knees.
And don't I lead them
like a good shepherd?
I stand at the sink,
where the water is still
overflowing the pot,
turn off the faucet,
then heat the water and sit down.
After the last sweet mouthful of chocolate
burns its way down my throat,
I open the library book,
the one on mythology,
and begin to read.
Saturn, it says, devours his children.
Yes, it's true, I know it.
An ordinary man, though, a man like me
eats and is full.
Only God is never satisfied.

THE MOTHER'S TALE

Once when I was young, Juanito,
there was a ballroom in Lima
where Hernán, your father,
danced with another woman
and I cut him across the cheek
with a pocketknife.
Oh, the pitch of the music sometimes,
the smoke and rustle of crinoline.
But what things to remember now
on your wedding day.
I pour a kettle of hot water
into the wooden tub where you are sitting.
I was young, free.
But Juanito, how free is a woman?—
born with Eve's sin between her legs,
and inside her,
Lucifer sits on a throne of abalone shells,
his staff with the head of John the Baptist
skewered on it.
And in judgment, son, in judgment he says
that women will bear the fruit of the tree
we wished so much to eat
and that fruit will devour us
generation by generation,

so my son,
you must beat Rosita often.
She must know the weight of a man's hand,
the bruises that are like the wounds of Christ.
Her blood that is black at the heart
must flow until it is as red and pure as His.
And she must be pregnant always
if not with child
then with the knowledge
that she is alive because of you.
That you can take her life
more easily than she creates it,
that suffering is her inheritance from you
and through you, from Christ,
who walked on his mother's body
to be the King of Heaven.

THE PRIEST'S CONFESSION

1

I didn't say mass this morning.
I stood in the bell tower
and watched Rosamund, the orphan,
chase butterflies, her laughter
rising, slamming into me,
while the almond scent of her body
wrapped around my neck like a noose.
Let me go, I told her once,
you'll have to let me go,
but she held on.
She was twelve.
She annoyed me,
lying in her little bed—
Tell me a story, Father,
Father, I can't sleep. I miss my mother.
Can I sleep with you?
I carried her into my room—
the crucifix, the bare white walls.
While she slept,
she threw the covers back.
Her cotton gown was wedged above her thighs.
I nearly touched her.
I prayed for deliverance, but none came.
Later, I broke my rosary.

The huge, black wooden beads
clattered to the floor
like ovoid marbles,
and I in my black robe,
a bead on God's own broken rosary,
also rolled there on the floor
in a kind of ecstasy.
I remembered how when I was six
Lizabeta, the witch, blessed me,
rocking in her ladder-back chair,
while I drank pig's blood
and ate it smeared across a slice of bread.
She said, *Eat, Emilio, eat.*
Hell is only as far as your next breath
and heaven unimaginably distant.
Gate after gate stands between you and God,
so why not meet the devil instead?
He at least has time for people.
When she died, the villagers
burned her house.

I lay my hand on the bell.
Sometimes when I ring this,
I feel I'll fragment,
then reassemble
and I'll be some other thing—
a club to beat,
a stick to heave at something:
between the act and the actor
there can be no separateness.
That is Gnostic. Heresy.

Lord, I crave things,
Rosamund's bird's nest of hair
barely covered by her drawers.
I want to know that you love me,
that the screams of men,
as loud as any trumpet,
have brought down the gates of stone
between us.

2

The next four years,
Rosamund's breasts grew
and grew in secret
like two evil thoughts.
I made her confess to me
and one night, she swooned,
she fell against me
and I laid her down.
I bent her legs this way and that.
I pressed my face between them
to smell "Our Lady's Roses"
and finally, I wanted to eat them.
I bit down, her hair was like thorns,
my mouth bled, but I didn't stop.
She was so quiet,
then suddenly she cried out
and sat up;
her face, a hazy flame,
moved closer and closer to mine,
until our lips touched.
I called her woman then

because I knew what it meant.
But I call you God, the Father,
and you're a stranger to me.

3
I pull the thick rope
from the rafter
and roll it up.
I thought I'd use this today,
that I'd kick off the needlepoint footstool
and swing out over the churchyard
as if it were the blue and weary Earth,
that as I flew out into space,
I'd lose my skin, my bones
to the sound of one bell
ringing in the empty sky.
Your voice, Lord.
Instead, I hear Rosamund's laughter,
sometimes her screams,
and behind them, my name,
calling from the roots of trees,
flowers, plants,
from the navel of Lucifer
from which all that is living
grows and ascends toward you,
a journey not home,
not back to the source of things,
but away from it,
toward a harsh, purifying light
that keeps nothing whole—
while my sweet, dark Kyries
became the wine of water

and I drank you.
I married you,
not with my imperfect body,
but with my perfect soul.
Yet, I know I'd have climbed
and climbed through the seven heavens
and found each empty.

I lean from the bell tower.
It's twilight;
smoke is beginning to gray the sky.
Rosamund has gone inside
to wait for me.
She's loosened her hair
and unbuttoned her blouse
the way I like,
set table,
and prayed,
as I do—
one more night.
Lamb stew, salty butter.
I'm the hard, black bread on the water.
Lord, come walk with me.

ELEGY

for my cousin John, 1946–1967

Hundreds of flies
rise from my face
and I feel as if I'm flying.
But it's only a daydream.
I'm seventy-five,
in the veterans' hospital
and this isn't 1917.
On TV, Saigon is splitting apart
like a cheap Moroccan leather suitcase
and we are leaving it all behind;
our dirty, dirty laundry.
Maybe it's the right thing to do.
Maybe soldiers are reborn infinitely
to do each century's killing and mopping up.
We stand at attention in full dress.
A general rides by in an open car
and we cheer. How I cheered.
Here's to the trenches, the mud,
the bullet-riddled days and nights,
that one night in November 1917,
when I thought I was dead,
when I felt myself rising
straight for the moon's green, cheesy heart.
But I wasn't dead,
I was on a troop ship in the English Channel
twenty-seven years later
and nothing had changed.

Last night, I dreamed about my mother.
She was pregnant with me
and I was also there with her
as a young man.
I wanted to end it inside her womb
with my bayonet.
And somehow, I cut my way to the child.
I took him by the feet
and flung him high
over a smoky black rainbow.

2

Suddenly, my body jerks forward, then back
and just as suddenly,
the TV screen darkens
and the voices of the journalists fade,
then hang in the air like whispers,
as the orderly takes hold of my wheelchair.
When we move down the hallway,
small, almond-eyed people
cheer as I roll by.
I recognize them all:
that one was with me in the trenches,
that one in the concentration camp,
and that vapor there from Nagasaki.
The orderly lifts me into bed
and folds the mended blanket across my chest.
Imagining things, I say to him.
Well, what if I am?—
just lower the coffin.
Let those clods of earth come down
like a hundred blows.

You say never you, never,
but when it's your turn,
you'll pack your sweet dreams
in your old kit bag and go.
And on that true last day,
you and I will rise toward heaven
like two great brass notes
from Gabriel's horn.
We'll shout, *Hallelujah,*
the war is over.
We'll shout the gates
of heaven down.

THE TESTIMONY OF
J. ROBERT OPPENHEIMER

A Fiction

When I attained enlightenment,
I threw off the night like an old skin.
My eyes filled with light
and I fell to the ground.
I lay in Los Alamos,
while at the same time,
I fell
toward Hiroshima,
faster and faster,
till the earth,
till the morning
slipped away beneath me.
Some say when I hit
there was an explosion,
a searing wind that swept the dead before it,
but there was only silence,
only the soothing baby-blue morning
rocking me in its cradle of cumulus cloud,
only rest.
There beyond the blur of mortality,
the roots of the trees of Life and Death,
the trees William Blake called Art and Science,
joined in a kind of Gordian knot
even Alexander couldn't cut.
To me, the ideological high wire
is for fools to balance on with their illusions.

It is better to leap into the void.
Isn't that what we all want anyway?—
to eliminate all pretense
till like the oppressed who in the end
identifies with the oppressor,
we accept the worst in ourselves
and are set free.

In high school, they told me
all scientists
start from the hypothesis "what if"
and it's true.
What we as a brotherhood lack in imagination
we make up for with curiosity.
I was always motivated
by a ferocious need to know.
Can you tell me, gentlemen,
that you don't want it too?—
the public collapse,
the big fall smooth as honey down a throat.
Anything that gets you closer
to what you are.
Oh, to be born again and again
from that dark, metal womb,
the sweet, intoxicating smell of decay
the imminent dead give off
rising to embrace me.

But I could say anything, couldn't I?
Like a bed we make and unmake at whim,
the truth is always changing,
always shaped by the latest

collective urge to destroy.
So I sit here,
gnawed down by the teeth
of my nightmares.
My soul, a wound that will not heal.
All I know is that urge,
the pure, sibylline intensity of it.
Now, here at parade's end
all that matters:
our military in readiness,
our private citizens
in a constant frenzy of patriotism
and jingoistic pride,
our enemies endless,
our need to defend infinite.
Good soldiers,
we do not regret or mourn,
but pick up the guns of our fallen.
Like characters in the funny papers,
under the heading
"Further Adventures of the Lost Tribe,"
we march past the third eye of History,
as it rocks back and forth
in its hammock of stars.
We strip away the tattered fabric
of the universe
to the juicy, dark meat,
the nothing beyond time.
We tear ourselves down atom by atom,
till electron and positron,
we become our own transcendent annihilation.

THE DETECTIVE

I lie on my daughter's body
to hold her in the earth,
but she won't stay;
she rises, lifting me with her,
as if she were air
and not some remnant
of failed reeducation
in a Cambodian mass grave.
We rise, till I wake.
I sit up, turn on the lamp,
and stare at the photo of the girl
who died yesterday,
at her Vietnamese mother
and her American father.
Jewel van duc Thompson,
murdered in Springfield, Ohio,
in her eighteenth year,
gone the day she was born
like in the cartoons,
when somebody rolls up the road
that stretches into the horizon
and the TV screen goes black . . .

Go home, Captain,
the cop said yesterday,
as he gripped my hand
and hauled himself

up from the ditch
where they'd found her
like Persephone
climbing from the underworld
one more time,
his eyes bright,
the hunger for life
and a good time
riding his back like a jockey.
Death is a vacation, I answered.
Then my hand was free
and I could see
how she was thrown
from the highway
down the embankment.
Where were Art and Rationality
when it counted? I thought—
always around the corner
from somebody else's street.
Even the ice cream man
never, ever made your block,
though you could hear the bells,
though you could feel the chill
like a shock
those hot days
when your company beat the bushes,
when you bit into death's chocolate-covered center
and froze . . .

I turn off the lamp
and lie still in the dark.
Somewhere in time, it is 1968.

I am bending over a wounded man
with my knife.
My company calls me the Angel of Mercy.
I don't remember yesterday
and there is no tomorrow.
There is only the moment
the knife descends
from the equatorial dark.
Only a step
across the Cambodian border
from Vietnam
to search and destroy the enemy,
but it is just a short time
till the enemy discovers me
and I would die,
but for the woman
who takes me to the border,
who crosses with me from the underworld
back to the underworld.
I open the curtain.
Outside, the early morning
is spinning, gathering speed,
and moving down the street
like a whirlwind.
I pull the curtain shut again
and switch on my tape
of the murderer's confession,
hear the faint, raspy voice
playing and replaying itself.
It was Saturday night.
She stood alone at the bus stop.
When she took the first step

toward my car,
I dropped the key once, twice.
She smiled, she picked it up.
I lie back on the bed,
while the voice
wears itself out.
Yes, I think,
you live for a while.
You get tired.
You walk the road into the interior
and never come back.
You disappear
the way the woman
and your child disappear
into Cambodia
in the pink light of dawn,
early April 1975.
You say you'll go back,
but you never do.
Springfield, Phnom Penh.
So many thousands of miles
between a lie and the truth.
No, just a step.
The murderer's voice rises,
becomes shrill.
Man, he says, *is it wrong*
to do what is necessary?
I switch off the tape.
Each time I sit down,
I think I won't get up again;
I sink through the bed, the floor,
and out the other side of the Earth.

There my daughter denounces me.
She turns me back
at the muddy border of forgiveness.
I get up, dress quickly,
then open the curtain wide.

At the door,
I put my hand on the knob, hesitate,
then step out into sunlight.
I get into the car,
lift the key to the ignition,
drop it.
My hand is shaking.
I look into the back seat.
The Twentieth Century is there,
wearing a necklace of grenades
that glitters against its black skin.
I stare, see the pins
have all been pulled.
Drive, says the voice.
I turn to the wheel,
imagine the explosions,
house after house
disintegrating in flames,
but all is silent.
People go on with their lives
on this day that is one hundred years long,
on this sad red balloon of a planet,
the air escaping from it
like the hot, sour breath of a child.

THE JOURNALIST

1

In the old photograph,
I'm holding my nose
and my friend Stutz
has a finger down his throat.
We're sixteen, in Cedar Falls.
It's all still a joke.
In my mind, I'm back there.
The woman who used me
like a dirty rag is gone
in a red convertible.
The top is down.
She sits beside the Greek
from out of town,
his hair slicked down
with bergamot.
I don't care, I do care
that she cruises the streets
of Little America without me.
I take a last drag off my Lucky,
pull my cap low,
and take the old road to the fairground.
I'm sixteen. What do I know
about love and passion, I think,
as I watch the circus set up,
watch as the elephants pitch and sway,

heads and trunks swinging wildly.
When the yellow leaves stir
and spin around me,
I walk back to the river
and skim stones
across the clear, gold water
of early evening,
till the 7:18 whistle blows.
Then as if on command,
I start running from childhood,
from the hometown
that keeps me a boy
when I want to be a man.
Manhood, a dream, an illusion, I think,
as I lay down the photograph
and stand still in the anemic glow
of the darkroom lights,
my body giving off the formaldehyde smell
of the unknown.

2

In Vietnam in 1966,
I stood among the gathering crowd,
as the Buddhist nun
doused her robe with gasoline.
As an American, I couldn't understand
and as I stood there,
I imagined myself
moving through the crowd
to stop her, but I didn't.
I held my camera in position.
Then it happened so quickly—

her assistant stepped forward
with a match.
Flames rose up the nun's robe
and covered her face,
then her charred body
slowly fell to the ground.
That year in Vietnam,
I threw my life in the air
like a silver baton.
I could catch it with my eyes closed.
Till one night,
it sailed into black space like a wish
and disappeared.
Or was it me who vanished,
sucking the hard rock candy
of the future,
sure that a man's life is art,
that mine had to be?
But tonight, I'm fifty-three.
I've drunk my way to the bottom
of that river of my youth
and I'm lying there
like a fat carp,
belly-down in the muck.
And nothing, not the blonde,
the red car,
or the smell of new money,
can get me up again.

I lay out the photographs of the nun.
I remember how her assistant
spoke to the crowd,

how no one acknowledged her,
how we stood another two or three minutes,
till I put my hand in my pocket,
brought out the matchbook,
and threw it to the nun's side.
I stare at the last photograph—
the nun's heart that would not burn,
the assistant, her hand stretched toward me
with the matchbook in it.
What is left out?—
a man, me, stepping forward,
tearing off a match, striking it
and touching it to the heart.
I throw the photographs
in the metal wastebasket,
then take the nun's heart
from the glass container of formaldehyde.
I light a match.
Still the heart won't burn.
I put the fire out,
close my eyes
and see myself running,
holding a lump
wrapped in a handkerchief.
I think someone will stop me
or try to, but no one does.
I open my eyes,
take the heart,
and hold it against my own.
When I was sixteen,
I was the dutiful son.
I washed my hands,

helped my mother set the table,
got my hair cut, my shoes shined.
I tipped the black man
I called "boy" a dime.
I didn't excel,
but I knew I could be heroic
if I had to.
I'd set the sharp end
of the compass
down on blank paper
and with the pencil end
I was drawing the circle
that would contain me—
everything I wanted,
everything I'd settle for.
Life and all its imitations.
That day in Hue,
I had the chance to step
from the circle
and I took it.
But when I turned back,
everything inside it was burning.
My past was gone. I was gone.
But the boy was still there.
He watched the flames take the nun.
He took her heart. He was running.
I was bound, he said to himself, *I'm free.*
But it was a lie.

I put the heart back in the container,
hear the heavy footsteps
of my wife, the blonde,

who is gray now,
who is clumping up the stairs
in her rubber boots
like some female Santa Claus.
In the heavy canvas bag
slung over her shoulder—
all the smashed toys of my life.
Wait, I say, as I stand
with my shoulder against the door.
Wait. You haven't heard
the best part yet—
A boy is running away from home.
He's lost his cap.
He's wearing the icy wind
like an overcoat.
He can't go back. He won't go back.
He never left.

FATE

[1991]

GO

for Mary Jo Kopechne and Edward Kennedy

Once upon a Massachusetts midnight,
under a sky smoothed of light,
as if wiped by flannel,
a car sailed off a bridge
but did not float.
Then the water, the dark gray water,
opened its mouth
and I slid down its throat.
But when it tried to swallow
the man they call my lover *and* my killer,
it choked and spat him back into your faces.
He carried no traces of me on his body
or in his heart,
but the part I played in his destruction
made me worthy of all of Shakespeare's villains.
Yet why doesn't somebody
tear me from the bit player's cold embrace
and let me set the stage on fire,
dressed up in revisionists' flesh?
Why doesn't someone write the monologue
that will finally explain this melodrama
and let me claim it?
Let me perform my own exorcism
as I performed the music of my dying
to someone else's rhythm.
Give 'em a show, Mary Jo Kopechne,
the one they really paid to see.

Bring down the house of Kennedy for good,
or, like Jehovah, re-create it in its soiled image.
I don't know. I don't know.
What scene is this, what act?
How did I miss the part where I enter to applause,
where the prince of make-believe
is waiting beside the hearse,
all its doors thrown open?
But right here in the script
somebody's written *Enter* beside the word *Exit*
and under that *You Choose.*
But when I do,
a human wall closes round me
and I can't get to you, Teddy,
behind your friends,
their arms raised to fend off blows,
even my own parents, with chests bared
to take for you any condemnation
aimed like a bullet.
If I shove those dominoes, will they fall
while I go marching in,
some Satchmo who'll blow the walls
of this Jericho of lies down?
But this aside's too complicated,
too weighed by metaphors and similes.
All right, I'll say it plainly.
Jack or Bobby would have died with me.
Think of publicity, the headlines—
you'd have been a hero.
Instead you caught your media resurrection
in your teeth and let it go.

You dove and dove
for that woman
so often reduced by the press
to just breasts and Mound of Venus,
but I broke free of all that.
I found another kind of ecstasy.
I'd always thought my only calling
would be acquiescent mate,
but goodness doesn't count
among self-made nobility,
especially the Irish Catholic ones.
What does is the pose of sacrifice,
so I swam deeper and deeper down,
hoping you'd understand and follow,
but each time you rose for air,
you sucked it like a child at breast.
It should have been mine,
full of death's sweet buttermilk,
but yes, you broke the skin of water
one last time,
you climbed onto Dyke Bridge
alive, but dead to the world.
If only you'd realized it.

How ironic that from your stained integrity
came the conscience of what's left
of the Democratic party,
brought to its knobby knees by Mistress Fortune.
You have earned that,
you who've grown fat and jowly
at the table where no feast is ever served,

just sparkling water with a twist of lime,
where once a glass of gin and tonic stood,
a good son's hands about to raise it in a toast
in praise of brothers.
Sometimes, stunned, you ask the dark
beyond the footlights
what happened to that life.
Other times, you slowly strip
to a Bessie Smith blues song,
you know the one about dues
and jelly, always jellyroll,
or you play the old magic trick—
a member of the audience holds up
an object from your past
and you identify it with charades.
But if you'd only ask me,
I'd erase those lines you've drawn on air
and deconstruct my own unfinished masterpiece,
a family portrait
of one man
and one true wife,
who, though the race was lost long ago,
stands behind him
with a starting gun
as he forever runs and runs in place.

JIMMY HOFFA'S ODYSSEY

I remember summers
when the ice man used to come,
a hunk of winter
caught between his iron tongs,
and in the kitchen, my ma with a rag,
wiping the floor when he'd gone;
sweet song of the vegetable man
like the music
a million silver dollars make,
as they jingle, jangle
in that big pocket of your dreams.
Dreams. Yes, and lies.
When I was a boy, I hauled ashes
in a wagon,
pulled by a bony horse
not even good enough for soap,
so later, when they called me
stocky little dockworker
with my slicked-back black hair,
my two-tone shoes, cheap suits,
and fat, smelly cigars,
I didn't care.
I had my compensation.
Bobby Kennedy didn't want to understand,
but to the teamsters back in '58 . . .
I had 'em all in my pocket then,

statesmen, lawyers, movie stars,
Joe Louis, for God's sake.
For a time, I won spin after spin
on the tin wheel of fate,
but in the end, like those glory boys
Jack and Bobby,
I was only icing on the sucker cake.

I know the alibis, the lies,
stacked up like bodies
on a gurney going nowhere,
but Hoffa went, he went
walking in a parking lot one day,
while he waited for a so-called
friend, a peacemaker, ha.
See him there, bored and sweating.
See the car roll toward him
as he does a little dance, a polka step or two,
when the doors open
and the glare of sunlight off a windshield
becomes so bright
that he is blinded by it.
Later, I come to,
while a blue broccoli-looking creature
is taking tubes from my arms and legs.
Then he walks me round and round
till I can stand on my own.
He talks to me through some machine,
tells me I'm on a spaceship,
tells me he's lonely,
then he sits me down at the controls,

he talks to me about his life in some galaxy
whose name I can't pronounce.
I become a confidant of sorts, a friend,
until one day outside Roswell, New Mexico,
his skin begins to rot,
so I start collecting specimens for him:
rocks, bugs, plants,
my walks taking me farther and farther
till I find this abandoned gas station,
and when he dies,
I put up signs along the highway,
the ones that say, "10 miles, 5, 1 mile
to see THE THING!"
And fifty cents for kids, a dollar for adults,
buys a glimpse of a spaceman
in an airtight case
and Hoffa on the other side of the glass,
Hoffa who chooses to let everybody think
he was pulverized in some New Jersey nightmare.
I drink an Orange Crush, prop my feet up,
and watch the sun go down,
the moon come up. A year goes by like this,
two, when suddenly it's not enough.
In a rage, I smash the case
and burn down the shack
with the spaceman inside.
I hitch a ride to town and take a job
at McDonald's,
and when I raise enough cash,
take a Greyhound to Detroit,
but in the station,

as if commanded by a force outside myself,
buy a ticket back.
In the desert once again, I board the spaceship
and take off,
and one night,
kidnap two hunters in Maine,
later, a family in Texas,
a telephone lineman in upstate New York.
I want to tell them who I am,
but all I do is mumble, stare, and touch them,
as if I'd never been a man among men,
when the dollar sign was a benediction.
Instead of words what comes are images
of Hoffa smacked in the head
so hard he hurls himself forward,
then slams back in the seat,
and later, shot through each eye, each ear,
his mouth,
his body heaved in a trash compactor
and to its whir, whine, and moan,
crushed beyond anger.
Again and again, I play memory games
in the casino of the past.
Yes, half a chance,
I'd do it all the same,
so aim that pistol, wise guy,
and fire and keep on firing.
Let me go, let me go,
but give the bosses of the world,
the brass-assed monkeys
who haven't paid the price in blood,

this warning:
sometime when they are least expecting,
I am coming back
to take my place on the picket line,
because, like any other union man,
I earned it.

BOYS AND GIRLS, LENNY BRUCE,
OR BACK FROM THE DEAD

for Willem Dafoe, Ron Vawter, and the Wooster Group

1

So how's it going, folks?—
broke, exhausted,
shtuped and duped again.
You can take it.
Hell, the meaning of life
is taking it,
in the mouth, the ass, the—
o-o-o-h
it feels so good.
All together now, stand up, bend over,
and say *a-a-a-h*.
Now sit down, relax, enjoy the show
that asks the magic question,
with such a stink,
can shit be far behind?
But no, what you smell is an odor
of another kind,
fear, disgust, plus all the things
you don't want to hear,
the things that drive you
from the club,
a body, a name, and nothing more.
Alone, on stage, I take
what you have left behind
and wear it like a wide, gaudy tie,

a sight gag
for the next show,
when I'll pick at some other scab
until it bleeds,
until that blood turns to wine
and we get drunk
on the incomprehensible
raison d'être of our lives.

2

I address myself
most often to guys,
because guys are least
able to express themselves.
You women know that.
You've read it in *Ms.* and *Cosmo.*
I am not a woman hater;
I'm a woman baiter, I like
to argue, I like confrontation
as long as I win,
but you women make it hard,
you don't play by rules
but by emotions.
One minute you're devoted,
the next you've placed
an ad in *New York* magazine
that says we're impotent.
Know what I'm saying?
You women tell each other things
a guy does not want told.
You hold these secret sessions
over coffee and croissants.

We disappear in your complaints,
and in our places, those things
you've created.
So guys, I advise let 'em know
you won't be violated,
you won't be changed
into their tormentor.
You women out there,
all I'm trying to say,
in the end,
we're only bad impersonations
of our fantasies.
Just let the accusation waltz be ended,
not the dance.

3

I tried to reach
that state of grace
when performer and audience fuse,
but each show left a hunger
even sex couldn't satisfy.
The closest thing—
heroin. No,
like the Velvet Underground sang it—
her-row-in.
Shot, snorted, smoked,
even laced with sugar
and spread on cereal for breakfast.
But I was cool, it was cool,
until one night I thought
to hell with this moderation shit.
I took one needle too many

in that last uncollapsed vein,
that trail up the cold Himalayas.
I climbed and climbed
and finally it was just me
and the abominable snowman,
starring in my own *Lost Horizon*.
I had *arrived*
to Miles playing background trumpet.
Ice encased me from the neck down;
the snowman never moved,
never made a sound,
maybe he wasn't even there,
maybe he was the pure air of imagination.
That's o–x–y–g–e–n.
I breathed faster
and faster, then slow
and let it all come down,
but that was just before
the floor, the Hollywood
night and smog,
the quick trip to the morgue
to identify
someone I used to know.
He looked like me, he was
me,
but in some other form
or incarnation,
my rib cage cut open, my guts
bluish gray and shriveled,
liver going black,
heart too,
my dick sucked back inside,

as if through a straw or tube.
I lay like that for days
while they hunted me for drugs,
as if prospecting gold
and that gold was my disgrace,
but now I'm back
to claim my share of whatever's
left out there among the ruins.
And on stage,
under the white-hot spotlights,
give it all I've got.
So greetings from the reclamation zone.
Like Christmas, it was bound to come,
and like some hostage savior,
I'm here to stay
till everybody's sanctified
in laughter.
That's right, it's not your balls, your pussy,
or your money
that I'm after; it's your soul.

GENERAL GEORGE ARMSTRONG
CUSTER: MY LIFE IN THE THEATER

After the blood wedding
at Little Big Horn,
I rose from death,
a bride loved past desire
yet unsatisfied,
and walked among the mutilated corpses.
Skin stripped from them,
they were as white as marble,
their raw scalps like red bathing caps.
Sometimes I bent to stroke the dying horses
as dew bathed my feet.
When I tore the arrows from my genitals,
I heard again the sound of the squaws.
The trills on their tongues thrilled me.
Those sounds were victory
and I was victory's slave
and she was a better lover than my wife
or the colored laundress
I took under a wagon one night
when I was hot with my invincibility.
Why, eventually even Sitting Bull
joined a Wild West show.
He rode a dancing pony
and sold his autograph to anyone who'd pay
and I might have become president,
my buckskin suit, white hat,

two guns, and rifle
flung in some closet
while I wore silk shirts
and trousers made of cotton
milled on my own shores
and took my manly pleasures
with more accomplished whores.
Instead I dress in lies and contradictions
and no one recognizes me.
All they see is the tall, skinny mercenary
with yellow hair
and blue, vacant eyes that stare,
so while I chew the tips of my mustache,
the cameras pass over me.
The journalists interview that guy or that one
and I want to shoot them down,
but that's been done before
by some back-door assassin or other
who kills publicly for sport,
but I kill for
the spectacle, the operatic pitch
of the little civil wars
that decimate from inside,
as in Belfast, Beirut, or Los Angeles,
where people know how it feels to be
somebody's personal Indian,
a few arrows, a few bullets short of home,
then left behind to roam this afterlife.
Once I knelt on one knee,
firing from my circle of self-deceit,
no thought but to extinguish thought,
until I brought down each brave,

but it was his red hand that wounded me,
no matter how many times I shot,
clubbed, clawed, or bit him,
my mouth overflowing with blood,
the rubbery flesh I chewed
that left no evidence of my savagery.
When I raised the gun to my own head,
I recalled the fields and fields of yellow flowers
that lit my way as I rode to battle.
How beautiful they were,
how often I stopped to pick them.
I twined them in my horse's mane
and in my hair,
but they were useless amulets
that could not stop my bullet
as it sizzled through flesh, then bone.
Now misfortune's soldier,
black armband on sleeve and hand on heart,
I pledge no fear
as chance propels me
into another breach
from which there is no deliverance,
only the tragicomedy of defeat acted out
in the belly of the cosmic whale,
where I swim against the dark, relentless tide.

INTERVIEW WITH A POLICEMAN

You say you want this story
in my own words,
but you won't tell it my way.
Reporters never do.
If everybody's racist,
that means you too.
I grab your finger
as you jab it at my chest.
So what, the minicam caught that?
You want to know all about it, right?—
the liquor store, the black kid
who pulled his gun
at the wrong time.
You saw the dollars he fell on and bloodied.
Remember how cold it was that night,
but I was sweating.
I'd worked hard, I was through
for twenty-four hours,
and I wanted some brew.
When I heard a shout,
I turned and saw the clerk
with his hands in the air,
saw the kid drop his gun
as I yelled and ran from the back.
I only fired when he bent down,
picked up his gun, and again dropped it.
I saw he was terrified,

saw his shoulder and head jerk to the side
as the next bullet hit.
When I dove down, he got his gun once more
and fired wildly.
Liquor poured onto the counter, the floor
onto which he fell back finally,
still firing now toward the door,
when his arm flung itself behind him.
As I crawled toward him,
I could hear dance music
over the sound of liquor spilling and spilling,
and when I balanced on my hands
and stared at him, a cough or spasm
sent a stream of blood out of his mouth
that hit me in the face.

Later, I felt as if I'd left part of myself
stranded on that other side,
where anyplace you turn is down,
is out for money, for drugs,
or just for something new like shoes
or sunglasses,
where your own rage
destroys everything in its wake,
including you.
Especially you.
Go on, set your pad and pencil down,
turn off the camera, the tape.
The ape in the gilded cage
looks too familiar, doesn't he,
and underneath it all,
like me, you just want to forget him.

Tonight, though, for a while you'll lie awake.
You'll hear the sound of gunshots
in someone else's neighborhood,
then, comforted, turn over in your bed
and close your eyes,
but the boy like a shark redeemed at last
yet unrepentant
will reenter your life
by the unlocked door of sleep
to take everything but his fury back.

JAMES DEAN

Night after night,
I danced on dynamite,
as light of foot as Fred Astaire,
until I drove the road
like the back of a black panther,
speckled with the gold
of the cold and distant stars
and the slam, bang, bam
of metal jammed against metal.
My head nearly tore from my neck,
my bones broke in fragments
like half-remembered sentences,
and my body,
as if it had been beaten
by a thousand fists,
bruised dark blue;
yet a breath entered my wide-open mouth
and the odor of sweet grass
filled my nose. I died,
but the cameras kept filming
some guy named James,
kept me stranded among the so-called living,
though if anybody'd let me,
I'd have proved
that I was made of nothing
but one long, sweet kiss
before I wasn't there.

Still, I wear
my red jacket, blue jeans.
Sometimes I'm an empty space in line
at some Broadway cattle call,
or a shadow on a movie screen;
sometimes I caress a woman in her dreams,
kiss, undress her anyplace,
and make love to her
until she cries.
I cry out
as she squeezes me tight
between her thighs,
but when she grabs my hair,
my head comes off in her hands
and I take the grave again.
Maybe I never wanted a woman
as much as that anyway,
or even the spice of man on man
that I encountered once or twice,
the hole where I shoved myself,
framed by an aureole of coarse hair.
By that twilight in '55,
I had devised a way
of living in between
the rules that other people make.
The bongos, the dance classes with Eartha Kitt,
and finally racing cars,
I loved the incongruity of it.
They used to say that I was always on
and couldn't separate myself
from the characters I played,
and if I hadn't died,

I'd have burned out anyway,
but I didn't give Quaker's shit, man,
I gave performances.
I even peed on the set of *Giant*—
that's right—
and turned around
and did a scene with Liz Taylor.
I didn't wash my hands first.
All the same, I didn't need an audience.
That's the difference
between an actor
and some sly pretender
who manipulates himself
up on the tarnished silver screen.
I didn't *do* method; I did James Dean.
Since then, the posters, photographs, biographies
keep me unbetrayed by age or fashion,
and as many shows a night as it's requested,
I reenact my passion play
for anyone who's interested,
and when my Porsche
slams into that Ford,
I'm doing one hundred eighty-six thousand
miles a second,
but I never leave the stage.

REUNIONS WITH A GHOST

for Jim

The first night God created was too weak;
it fell down on its back,
a woman in a cobalt blue dress.
I was that woman and I didn't die.
I lived for you,
but you don't care. You're drunk again,
turned inward as always.
Nobody has trouble like I do, you tell me,
unzipping your pants
to show me the scar on your thigh,
where the train sliced into you
when you were ten.
You talk about it with wonder and self-contempt,
because you didn't die
and you think you deserved to.
When I kneel to touch it,
you just stand there
with your eyes closed,
your pants and underwear bunched at your ankles.
I slide my hand up your thigh
to the scar and you shiver
and grab me by the hair.
We kiss, we sink to the floor,
but we never touch it,
we just go on and on tumbling through space
like two bits of stardust that shed no light,
until it's finished,

our descent, our falling in place.
We sit up. Nothing's different, nothing.
Is it love, is it friendship
that pins us down,
until we give in,
then rise defeated once more
to reenter the sanctuary of our separate lives?
Sober now, you dress,
then sit watching me
go through the motions of reconstruction—
reddening cheeks, eyeshadowing eyelids,
sticking bobby pins here and there.
We kiss outside
and you walk off, arm in arm with your demon.
So I've come through the ordeal of loving once again,
sane, whole, wise, I think as I watch you,
and when you turn back, I see in your eyes
acceptance, resignation,
certainty that we must collide from time to time.
Yes. Yes, I meant goodbye when I said it.

CAPTURE

And that's how I found him,
hoeing weeds
in his garden.
He was shirtless,
his pants rolled below his navel.
I stopped and watched
as he swung the hoe down
to cut the head from a dark red flower.
He looked up then and smiled
and said, "It's like that with men."
He was not handsome;
his face was too flawed for that,
but somehow that made him beautiful,
with his thin hawk's nose over full lips
and the deep lines
that sliced his forehead.
His eyes gleamed
like two pale green chips of ice.
I said, "I'm a stranger here."
"You haven't seen our lake then,
shall I take you there?" he asked.
"When?"
"Now," he said, dropping the hoe.
He began to walk faster and faster
and I had to run to catch up to him.
There was no trail,

but he strode on through bushes that pricked me
and past low-hanging branches
that caught my skirt. Tore my skirt.
Then we were there.
"Lake, lake," I cried, then laughed,
threw my head back
the way laborers and drunks do,
and roared, or tried to.
"It's a pond for children to wade in.
At home, at home *we* have a lake
you can swim in;
it takes a whole day to cross it."
He stood with his back to me;
he was oily with sweat
and he shone like some living metal.
He turned to me. "Swim.
Swim?" he said with a question mark.
"I haven't got a suit."
"Ha!" he said. "Ha,"
and rolled his pants up to his waist,
daring me,
then lowered them all the way down.
I covered my eyes, and when I looked
he was walking into the water.
"Modesty, that's your name," he said
over his shoulder.
"And yours?" I asked.
"I don't need a name.
I am what you see."
He laughed and slapped the water
with his long, thin hands.

Then he swam from one side to the other;
he floated on his back
and I watched him, of course I did,
and when he was done,
he lay in the sun,
surrendered to the sun and my eyes.
"Do I pass now?" he asked
as he came to stand in front of me.
Then he said, "Seen one lately?
It's a fine one," he went on,
taking his cock in his hands.
"Touch it."
I shook my head.
"Get you," he said and began to walk off,
but I grabbed his hard, smooth calves
and kissed them,
and with my tongue
licked my way down to his feet
and kissed each toe.
He sank down beside me,
took my face in his hands,
and lifted my head back.
Then he kissed me;
our tongues battered our teeth. Touched.
He raised my skirt with one hand,
pressed me back
and held me to the earth
with the weight of his body.
I bit his shoulder
as he pushed into me again. Again.
I kept my eyes open. He did too.

He stared and stared until he knew.
"You tricked me," he gasped
as he poured himself into my glass
and I drank him like *grappa*
made from grapes
I'd picked with my own hands.

EVIDENCE: FROM A
REPORTER'S NOTEBOOK

1

The city tosses and turns on the third rail
as the intern slams the clipboard on the desk.
He says, "We aren't finished with her yet."
"But Doc," I say, "maybe she's finished with you."
Schmoozing with an edge is what I call this.
He doesn't want the bruise of the six o'clock news
to blue-blacken his name by association.
He just wants someday to escape to a clinic
attached to a golf course
and drive his balls out
into the green bay it overlooks,
while back here, we all cook
in the same old grease
gone rancid from ceaseless poverty and crime.
"If I had a dime," he says, "if I had a dime . . ."
Then his voice trails off
and he stands and tries to swim
through the forty-foot waves
of three whole days and nights without sleep,
but each time, he's thrown back
on the hospital beach,
along with the dirty syringes, gauze,
and those who've drowned

in the contaminated water of their lives.
I say, "You know the hymn that goes,
'Some poor drowning, dying seaman
you may rescue, you may save'?"
"No," he shrugs, "it's more Charles Ives to me,
discord and disharmony
to go with all the inhumanity
that welcomes me each night
with open jaws and glistening teeth.
The victim, if she is one, is down the hall
and on the right. And this time, Maggie,
try to leave the way you came.
Don't make promises, or false claims of justice.
Let the lame stay lame,
don't set them dancing across the floor
in their own blood before they realize it."
"And what?" I say. "Go too far? But Doctor,
they're already there,
along with you and me, we need them,
they feed our superiority complexes.
You don't do Temple, I don't do Church,
but we've got faith, we're missionaries,
in search of some religion, some congregation
to place us in context,
even if it's someone else's.
And she *will* dance, as you and I will
and the TV viewers too,
to the fascinatin' rhythm of vaginal rape
and sodomization with a foreign object.
Hand me my tap shoes. I can't wait."

2

"You some reporter, right?" she says.
"It was a white man did this.
Said it is to show you niggers
who climbed from back of bus
to sit with us.
You nigger bitch, you get what you deserve,
and then he twist my arm behind me.
See the scratches, the splotches.
He drags me through some bushes and I got cuts.
You see 'em. You do.
He bit me too."
She tears at her skirt
and raises her knee, so I can see
high up her inner thigh,
too high, almost to knotted hair where underwear
of shiny fabric, nylon, I guess, begins.
"And when he finished with me," she says,
"he spit between my legs and rub it in."
I have learned not to wince
when such details are given;
still, I feel a slight
tightening of stomach muscles
before I make myself unclench
and do the true reporter thing,
which is to be the victim,
to relive with her again, again,
until it is my own night of degradation,
my own graduation from the shit to shit.
"Go on," she says, "write it down or somethin',
tape it, film it.

We got to hit him hard, hurt him. OK?"
"We will," I say, my smile in place now
like my hair, my friendship a brand-new dress
I wear until I wear it out or down,
but even as I take her hand extended to me,
so that we are banded together
in her stormy weather,
both without raincoats, umbrellas,
I flash on the report just read—
questionable rape, no tears, no bleeding there
or in the other place,
and bites that could be self-inflicted.
"Dirty sonofabitch," I say,
"is this United States of Revenge, or what?
We've got everything we need, got television,
and I have got your story
before the competition."

3

Six straight days, she's front-page news.
She makes guest appearances by dozens.
Everybody's cousin wants their piece
of tender meat,
but I've already eaten there
and I'm still hungry.
I'm suffocating too and I need air,
I need a long vacation from myself
and from my protégée
in all the ways manipulation pays,
when you play off the outrage
and the sympathy of others.

And she's a natural, she was born to do it,
should have her own byline in *New York Times,*
and I should have a Watergate,
should get my chance for Pulitzer glory,
but even Woodward faded like a paper rose
once he got his story.
I mean, you've got to know when to let it ride
and let it go, or else you wind up
some side show in Hackensack, or Tupelo.
You see, I couldn't prove that she was lying
and I couldn't prove she wasn't,
but that doesn't mean I abandoned her.
I swear the story led me somewhere else,
to the truth,
whatever that is, an excuse, I know, but valid.
Reality is a fruit salad anyway.
You take one bite, another, all those flavors,
which one is right?
She chose the role of victim
and for a while, I went along,
until tonight, when I look out
my window over Central Park
and think of other women whimpering
and bleeding in the darkness,
an infinity of suffering and abuse
to choose my next big winner from.
What I do, I take my own advice.
I whip my horse across the finish line
before I shoot it.
I step over her body
while the black sun rises behind me,
smoking like an old pistol.

The unofficial rules of this game
are that once found out,
you aim your tear-stained face into the camera.
You make your disgrace, your shame, work for you.
They don't burn bitches anymore,
they greet them at the back door with corsages
and slide them out the front into a reed basket
to float down the Nile, repentance,
into the arms of all us Little Egypts.
Welcome back.

4

My latest eyewitness news report,
focused on false accusations,
took as a prime example
my own delectable sample of the sport.
Even Warhol would have been proud,
would have remained in awe
long enough to list her name in his diaries,
might have understood her appetite,
have gained insight into her need,
though even her staunchest supporters
cannot explain away all contradictions,
all claims of violation that don't add up.
But really, if they only knew, in spite of that,
the lens through which we view the truth
is often cracked and filthy with the facts.
It could have happened. That is the bridge
that links the world of Kafka to us still,
the black pearl in pig's mouth
that won't be blasted out no matter what we do,
that finds us both on Oprah

or on Donahue, facing the packed pews
of the damned and the saved,
to send our innocence,
our guilt, across the crowded airwaves
to be filtered through
the ultimate democracy of TV,
which equalizes everything it sees
and freezes us to the screen between commercials
for movies of the week and shaving cream,
each show a rehearsal for the afternoon
when with a cry
she spreads her chocolate thighs
while I kneel down to look,
but still I find no evidence
of racist's or even boyfriend's semen.
I press my fingers hard against her,
then hold them up before the audience,
wet only with the thick spit of my betrayal.

THE COCKFIGHTER'S DAUGHTER

I found my father,
face down, in his homemade chili
and had to hit the bowl
with a hammer to get it off,
then scrape the pinto beans
and chunks of ground beef
off his face with a knife.
Once he was clean
I called the police,
described the dirt road
that snaked from the highway
to his trailer beside the river.
The rooster was in the bedroom,
tied to a table leg.
Nearby stood a tin of cloudy water
and a few seeds scattered on a piece of wax paper,
the cheap green carpet
stained by gobs of darker green shit.
I was careful not to get too close,
because, though his beak was tied shut,
he could still jump for me and claw me
as he had my father.
The scars ran down his arms to a hole
where the rooster had torn the flesh
and run with it,
finally spitting it out.
When the old man stopped the bleeding,

the rooster was waiting on top of the pickup,
his red eyes like Pentecostal flames.
That's when Father named him Preacher.
He lured him down with a hen
he kept penned in a coop,
fortified with the kind of grille
you find in those New York taxicabs.
It had slots for food and water
and a trap door on top,
so he could reach in and pull her out by the neck.
One morning he found her stiff and glassy-eyed
and stood watching
as the rooster attacked her carcass
until she was ripped
to bits of bloody flesh and feathers.
I cursed and screamed, but he told me to shut up,
stay inside, what did a girl know about it?
Then he looked at me with desire and disdain.
Later, he loaded the truck and left.
I was sixteen and I had a mean streak,
carried a knife
and wore such tight jeans I could hardly walk.
They all talked about me in town,
but I didn't care.
My hair was stringy and greasy and I was easy
for the truckers and the bar clowns
that hung around night after night,
fighting sometimes
just for the sheer pleasure of it.
I'd quit high school, but I could write my name
and add two plus two without a calculator.
And this time, I got to thinking,

I got to planning, and one morning
I hitched a ride
on a semi that was headed for California
in the blaze of a west Texas sunrise.
I remember how he'd sit reading
his schedules of bouts and planning his routes
to the heart of a country
he thought he could conquer with only one soldier,
the $1000 cockfight always further down the pike,
or balanced on the knife edge,
but he wanted to deny me even that,
wanted me silent and finally wife
to some other unfinished businessman,
but tonight, it's just me and this old rooster,
and when I'm ready, I untie him
and he runs through the trailer,
flapping his wings and crowing
like it's daybreak
and maybe it is.
Maybe we've both come our separate ways
to reconciliation,
or to placating the patron saint
of roosters and lost children,
and when I go outside, he strolls after me
until I kneel down and we stare at each other
from the cages we were born to,
both knowing what it's like
to fly at an enemy's face
and take him down for the final count.
Preacher, I say, I got my GED,
a AA degree in computer science,
a husband, and a son named Gerald, who's three.

I've been to L.A., Chicago,
and New York City on a dare, and know what?—
it's shitty everywhere, but at least it's not home.

After the coroner's gone, I clean up the trailer,
and later, smoke one of Father's
hand-rolled cigarettes
as I walk by the river,
a quivering way down in my guts,
while Preacher huddles in his cage.
A fat frog catches the lit cigarette
and swallows it.
I go back and look at the picture
of my husband and son,
reread the only letter I ever sent
and which he did not answer,
then tear it all to shreds.
I hitch the pickup to the trailer
and put Preacher's cage on the seat,
then I aim my car for the river, start it,
and jump out just before it hits.
I start the pickup and sit
bent over the steering wheel,
shaking and crying, until I hear Preacher
clawing at the wire,
my path clear,
my fear drained from me like blood from a cut
that's still not deep enough
to kill you off, Father,
to spill you out of me for good.
What was it that made us kin,
that sends daughters crawling after fathers

who abandon them at the womb's door?
What a great and liberating crowing
comes from your rooster
as another sunrise breaks the night apart
with bare hands
and the engine roars
as I press the pedal to the floor
and we shoot forward onto the road.
Your schedule of fights,
clipped above the dashboard,
flutters in the breeze.
Barstow, El Centro, then swing back
to Truth or Consequences, New Mexico,
and a twenty-minute soak in the hot springs
where Geronimo once bathed,
before we wind back again into Arizona,
then all the way to Idaho by way of Colorado,
the climb, then the slow, inevitable descent
toward the unknown
mine now. Mine.

GREED

[1993]

RIOT ACT, APRIL 29, 1992

I'm going out and get something.
I don't know what.
I don't care.
Whatever's out there, I'm going to get it.
Look in those shop windows at boxes
and boxes of Reeboks and Nikes
to make me fly through the air
like Michael Jordan
like Magic.
While I'm up there, I see Spike Lee.
Looks like he's flying too
straight through the glass
that separates me
from the virtual reality
I watch everyday on TV.
I know the difference between
what it is and what it isn't.
Just because I can't touch it
doesn't mean it isn't real.
All I have to do is smash the screen,
reach in and take what I want.
Break out of prison.
South Central homey's newly risen
from the night of living dead,
but this time he lives,

he gets to give the zombies
a taste of their own medicine.
Open wide and let me in,
or else I'll set your world on fire,
but you pretend that you don't hear.
You haven't heard the word is coming down
like the hammer of the gun
of this black son, locked out of the big house,
while massa looks out the window and sees only smoke.
Massa doesn't see anything else,
not because he can't,
but because he won't.
He'd rather hear me talking about mo' money,
mo' honeys and gold chains
and see me carrying my favorite things
from looted stores
than admit that underneath my Raiders' cap,
the aftermath is staring back
unblinking through the camera's lens,
courtesy of CNN,
my arms loaded with boxes of shoes
that I will sell at the swap meet
to make a few cents on the declining dollar.
And if I destroy myself
and my neighborhood
"ain't nobody's business, if I do,"
but the police are knocking hard
at my door
and before I can open it,
they break it down

and drag me in the yard.
They take me in to be processed and charged,
to await trial,
while Americans forget
the day the wealth finally trickled down
to the rest of us.

HOOVER, EDGAR J.

1

I'm the man behind the man
behind the man
and I have got my hands
in everybody's pockets.
I know who's been sticking his plug
in Marilyn Monroe's socket.
The shock it would give,
if everybody knew what King Arthur Jack
won't do to keep his rocket fueled.
I have files on everyone who counts,
yet they would amount to nothing,
if I did not have the will to use them.
Citizens must know their place,
but so must the president,
who simply decided one day
to hock his family jewels to the Mob.
They call me a cruel sonofabitch
just to aggravate me,
but my strength is truth.
I have the proof
of every kind of infidelity
and that makes me the one free man
in a country of prisoners
of lust, greed, hatred, need
greater than the fear of reprisal,

all the recognized sins
and all those unrecognizable,
except to me and God. Maybe God.
Sometimes my whole body aches
and I lie down on the floor,
just staring at the ceiling,
until I am feeling in control again,
my old confidence surging back
through me like electricity
and I get up, Frankenstein, revived
by the weakness of others
and as unstoppable as a handful of pills
that might kill you on a night like this,
like the night when Marilyn kissed it all goodbye.
It only came up roses after her show closed.
Too bad she had to row, row her boat
in lava lake.
They said they would make her a star.
Now far out in space,
her face big as a planet,
she looks down
on the whole pathetic, human race, wasting time,
as it shivers and shakes
down the conga line
behind Jack, Bobby, and me too.
When the voice on the phone
cried *"We're through"* and hung up,
she took an overdose,
trusting someone to save her,
but now she whispers,
"Honey, don't trust anybody
and never, ever fuck the head of state."

2

I had a head bald
as a licked clean plate
and a face . . .
Nobody ever said grace at my table,
yet, the god of judgment hovered over my head.
He led me down
dark halls to motel rooms,
where a locked door
and heavy perfume
could neither conceal, nor contain
the fumes of love that proclaimed
another fallen angel by his name.
Martin Luther King, Jr. preaches freedom,
but it means slavery for the white man.
It hands our keys to the robbers
and says, please, don't take anything.
Look at him on his knees
before pussy's altar.
Tomorrow with his wife beside him
he won't falter, as he shouts
from the pulpit about equality.
His words are a disease sweeping
through the colored people.
I can stop it if I choose.
I can release the tapes, the photographs
and end the so-called peaceful revolution,
but my solution is to sabotage discreetly,
to let someone else take the blame,
the Klan, or even another smoke,
who's younger and not broken in by privilege.

Someone like that Malcolm X,
that showstopping nigger,
who respects no boundaries
and hates the white man,
because he understands him.
He doesn't want to vote,
he doesn't want to tote that bail
in the name of integration.
He wants to sail back into blackness
and I say let him.
There is no such thing as freedom
and there never will be,
even for the white man.
The X-man knows it is eat, or be eaten
and Grandpa Hoover
has the biggest teeth.

3

They all wanted me
to take the A train to anonymity,
those who would seduce their own mothers,
after an audience with the Pope.
The Holy joke I call him.
I'd like to get a tape, or two,
of that crew in Rome.
A two-way mirror
somewhere in the Vatican, the camera rolling,
while some Cardinal is jerking off
over a silver bowl,
until his Vesuvius erupts again and again.
But I digress.

Now Lyndon Johnson and a negress,
that *is* delicious,
something best served on a platter.
Save it until after the elections
when it really matters.
I'm so scattered lately.
I feel like shattering all my Waterford crystal.
Ask me anything you want, but don't touch me.
I keep my pistol loaded.
Don't say I told you. Do.
I want the lowdown sonsofbitches
who betray me to know
I'm on to them like a fly on shit.
I will not rest,
until I spit in their mouths
and piss on their faces. The fools.
J. Edgar Hoover runs this country.
J. Edgar Hoover rules.

HOOVER TRISMEGISTUS

I rode the tail of a comet into the world.
Whether I were Edgar, or Mary
meant nothing to me.
I could be both, couldn't I?
That part was easy,
but what I couldn't tolerate
was the face in the bathroom mirror.
Was I a throwback to some buck
who sat hunched over in the hull
of a ship,
while the whip lashed his back?
"Do I look colored to you?" I ask Clyde,
who always, always turns aside my question,
as if he already knows the truth,
as if I have the proof in my possession
like a passport to destruction,
but a man who has fear on his side
can do anything.
Any dictator knows that.
You think Castro doesn't know it, or Chairman Mao?
There's a man I secretly admired.
We could have used a cultural revolution here.
Hell, we nearly had one.
The House un-American activities were a start,
but we didn't go far enough.
When they called Joe McCarthy's bluff,
he grabbed his nuts and ran

and the others banned together
to save their asses
anyway they could,
except for good old Roy Cohn,
a man after my own heart,
because he has none.
"Mary," he always tells me,
"what a red dress and high heels won't do
to lift a gal's spirits."
He's right.
When I have another one of my nightmares
of walking through high cotton
to a tree, where the boy swinging
at the end of a rope
opens his mouth and speaks to me,
saying, "One more nigger to go,"
I tell Roy to book that suite at the Plaza.
I know that Mississippi
is a state of mind we all carry in us
like a virus that activates
just when we think we're safe,
so of course, it isn't long
before I find my darker side
at a party up in Harlem.
He comes to me only once,
the love that twice dares not
speak its name.
See my divine black boy, fumbling with his zipper
while I wait impatiently,
hoping someone will see
that I am being had against my will
that I will deny the darkie inside me by killing him.

Still, he rises when he's done with me,
the gunshot would through his heart
still bleeding profusely,
the knife still protruding from his back.
In other words, he is my destiny.
Afterward, Roy arranges transportation for him,
plus a few dollars.
He tells him to chalk it up
to experience and let it be,
because there is no future in loving me.
I like *that*.
"You hear me, boy?" Roy asks him.
"Yes," he whispers.
"Yes, what?" asks Roy.
"Yes, sir!"
He may as well say, yes, master.
"Ask her," the boy says, meaning me,
"whether or not she is satisfied."
"Please," says Roy, "leave while you still can."
After that, my experiments in degradation
begin in earnest.
How many nights do I fight my desire
by giving in to it
and dreaming about him?
How many times do I pull down his pants
as he now swings from that rope,
only to find bloody holes,
where his genitals should be
and foiled again,
descend into the ship of myself,
where the slaves are jammed in so tightly,
all I can see is a mass of darkness,

not people,
though I can smell them,
though it is nothing compared
to the smell of my own fear,
because it's here I belong,
here on the endless crossing
into whiteness.

JACK RUBY ON ICE

"Shit, I heard they [Ruby and Oswald] were queer for each other."
—Double Cross, *Sam and Chuck Giancana*

A man needs ammunition,
because a bullet at the right time
accomplishes the ultimate divorce
and simplifies business.
I, myself, believe that force
allows the resolution of conflict.
I also believe in the right to bear arms
and the God-given right to settle scores,
but I did not measure my courage
by the size of my dick,
which I shook always after I peed,
so I would not stain my Jockeys,
though people claim I was careless
with my appearance
and kept a dirty apartment—
rolls of toilet paper strewn on the carpet,
along with cigar butts, wads of money,
condoms (so what?),
and other stuff too useless to name.
On that same floor, I lay with whores
without touching once,
if they were not clean,
if they had not washed
with hot water and Dial soap
that would not float like Ivory,
but was better for germs.

[*149*]

Imagine. A man stands trial among gentiles,
who regard him as the enemy,
a Jew they think will steal the pennies
off a dead man's eyes:
therefore, no one comes to his rescue.
Promises are broken.
I am not a man made in the image of my protectors,
so what do I get?—zilch.
Yet, I pay my debts, because I am a stand-up guy.
Even so, they song and dance me.
They light a powder keg under my feet,
which I must tell you always gave me trouble—
calluses, corns, bunions, toenails ingrown.
The chiropodist's office was my home away.
I spent a fortune just to be able
to walk without pain.
Still I could handle whatever came my way
and I can say that without a trace of shame.
A man can brag, if a man's aim is good enough.
But where was my glory,
where was my flag for wrapping in
when shots were fired
and the hired man collapsed
before the other hired man,
who once handed him cold cash
for services rendered
after Lee surrendered cherry like a bride?
Dream lover, he says, you are so mean.
I hit him, sure, not hard,
but just enough to make it rough and make him ready.
I am no fucking queer,
but a man, who enjoys the respect of other men.

I bend him over the couch, take out my strap
and whack his ass, then *him* I allow in my bed.
Afterward, I bathe him with these hands.
I lather him and wash him
the way a mother would a child.
My Lee was an adventurous boy.
One night, he even shows up with an MP,
the kind who calls you kike
and expects you to lick his spit-shined boots
and like it. I am as mad as hell at Lee.
He hits me back. First time.
The smile on his face like the day I shot him.
Next weekend, Ferrie the fairy arrives
and I have to put up with *his* craziness.
He brings a rat in a cage, gets drunk,
lets it out, sobers up. No rat.
He claims he's lost the cure for cancer.
I go out and buy another rat
and pretend I've found the other.
He cannot tell the difference.
Peace restored.
We turn to more pressing problems.
"People with an interest are asking
what we do about Lee," he says,
fixing me with what he thinks is a theatening stare.
"In competition, you know, sports, someone wins
and someone is eliminated."
I nod, no more.
"The door," he asks, "is closed on this then?"
"With a bang," I tell him.
When he's gone, I do some calculating.
I have troubles with the IRS.

There are threats to be met with action.
I am a man without regrets, yet, I know this thing
with Lee will not be easy to forget.
By now, he is like a son to me
and I am Abraham with no reprieve,
because unlike God,
men do not have the luxury of mercy.
So Lee becomes the patsy
and we dishonorable men
obey the first rule of self-preservation,
which is to find a fool to take the blame.
When it's him, or me
who needs a complicated explanation?
Another lone gunman has a plan,
but sometimes plans go awry.
He doesn't realize he, too, is a sacrifice,
until he smells his own flesh burning.

A president is taken by surprise
under the wide-open skies of Texas.
The kings of hearts cry,
"Off with Jack O'lantern's head,"
and two long days later,
I fill the chamber of my snub-nosed .38
with a silver bullet.
I am so patient, standing in the basement,
wearing a new shirt, tie, and suit,
old shoes, my favorite hat.
News is what I am going to make.
I will hand out interviews
as if they are doubloons

and replace Kennedy's and Oswald's faces.
When the elevator doors open,
I stride forward like a businessman
going to make the deal of a lifetime,
but all I do is seal my fate in concrete.
I do not even feel the trigger.
I am as numb as Lee is stunned by my betrayal.
The trap sprung at last, he passes into oblivion
and I pass gas from another bad meal
of pastrami and green onions
and the fact that my ass is now
on the griddle being done.
I am afraid my mask will slip
and I will tip the scales of justice
in the direction of the other assassins,
behind the rose-colored glass,
where Oswald and Ruby take the fall
and all the evidence is made to fit the crime,
at least until I've been abandoned by my friends.
Only then, I say, Chief Justice, I am in danger.
I will tell all if you arrange safe passage to D.C.,
but I receive a strange answer.
Can it be the Chief is a master of deception too?
The Chief says, "You do what's best."
My request for sanctuary is denied.
Now I am nothing but cancer cells.
Even my wife, Sheba, wouldn't recognize me.
So she is a dachshund?
She is the only woman good enough for me.
If only we could be together,
but I walk alone down a tunnel of white light,

then come out in a field of sunflowers,
their heads nodding hello, goodbye.
Some old acquaintances
whose names I can't remember
slap my back, then wander off
and I settle into an endless afternoon
without punishment, or reward
until a dark angel
in the guise of an evangelist
from Los Angeles appears
with the sword of justice in one hand
and a video camera in the other.
He offers me the chance to dance
on the graves of the slaves to the official story,
but why bother?
I bow my head over the edge of the precipice,
where the life I lead
lies dead in its own arms,
while the other victims of the resurrection
are stumbling toward an open car.
They are doomed to repeat the past,
but who can prove the truth
really isn't what you make it,
when it's so easy to fake?
Yet, his argument is so convincing that I waver.
I'll cooperate for one small favor, I tell him,
so we negotiate a detour on the road
to reopened files.
Now, on a city street,
paved with fool's gold,
I testify about the abuse of firearms

and the absolute power of lies,
then I take the few glistening coins from my hat
and throw them in the air.
They rise and rise, then fall back
on the eyes of America,
D-O-A inside a cardboard box.

OSWALD INCOGNITO &
ASTRAL TRAVELS

I've seen that face before,
staring at me
from the sixth floor
of the School Book Depository.
Is it déjà vu,
or is it the old story
of finally seeing yourself
in someone else's eyes?
Fake eyes, like the one
Sammy Davis Jr. wore
and used to slip into a stranger's glass of booze.
Once it got caught in somebody's throat.
They had to cut him open.
After Sammy washed it in boiling water,
he popped it back in.
He winked at himself in the mirror,
then he disappeared in a flash of gunfire
left over from the last hour of the assassin,
when three shots either narrowed, or widened, a plot,
depending on how you look at it,
not how it happened.
It wasn't easy being two places the same time,
but I managed the rarest of all magic tricks
with the flick of an eyelid,
I split down the middle,
I ran two directions,

but the lesson in this is
I ran in a circle,
came back where I started.
In my palm, a coin
was gleaming like twilight.
I dropped it down the slot
and got a Coke for my trouble.
The bubbles went up my nose.
I closed my eyes,
but that was no defense
against the magnificence of murder.
I admit to losing my perspective.
I couldn't see not only
that I had become ineffective,
but expendable,
so it was natural that the prime directive
would be to eliminate me.
Who could have predicted
that the shooter would be the man,
who kept boys as, uh, roommates,
who carried rolls of toilet paper
wherever he went as a talisman against disaster
sent straight to the bowels
and expelled with a howl of pleasure.
I'm only here to give voice
to what you've been thinking,
but were afraid to say in front of witnesses,
because they, too, could be the enemy
sent to do you in on TV,
which is itself a form of not being seen.
From the time I was a kid, I hid,
you know, in the back of my mind,

where it's cluttered with boxes of old comics,
whose heroes seduce children
into believing that evil and good
can be recognized by a kiss on the lips,
but my Judas pissed in his coffee,
before offering a sip.
It tasted like it always had,
slightly bitter, then sweet.
I knew what it meant
when Jack stepped from the shadows,
yet, I wanted to believe he was rescuing me.
I would take the gun
and in the best cowboy tradition,
go down in a hail of bullets,
In a split second, I imagined my hand
gripping the weapon,
but as I lay in the ambulance,
I understood the significance
of my death by deception.
Since I had only assumed the identity of myself,
it was somebody else who died,
who'd been saved by his unwitting defection from life.
Termination is, after all, a kind
of natural selection for spies.
It implies survival by escape
from the mass suicides of the pack.
Clowns like Jack Ruby move
through a crowd undetected,
but I am unprotected,
even my pubic hair isn't safe from scrutiny.
I'm not there either.
If I'm anywhere, I'm still trapped

in the palace of lies,
where I'm clothed in illusion
and fed confusion with a spoon.
I take the steps downstairs two-at-a-time.
I flip a penny to see if I should go.
Heads! I stay, but in a moment of panic,
I write my name on the wall
beside the Coke machine. OSWALD
in capital letters.
I erase it with spit and my shirttail,
but it keeps reappearing,
each time the letters get larger,
until the "O" is a hole
I can walk through
and when I finally do, it closes around me
like a mouth around the mouth of a rifle.
The question, though,
isn't what's in a name,
but what's in the barrel.
The answer is nothing,
but when I follow the arrow,
I find it pointing straight at me,
huddled beside a window,
as the president rides by unsuspecting,
only his eyes reflecting surprise
at the moment of impact.
Only one of his eyes breaks free of the socket
and is launched like a rocket,
while a man, shining shoes stops to listen,
as "Birth of the Blues" wafts down the alley,
from a club where Sammy is playing
to standing ovations.

"I need a vacation," Sammy thinks,
when a patron drinks the martini,
where the glass eye is hidden
among the olives and pearl onions
like a gunman on a grassy knoll.
Later, with my shoes buffed to a high sheen,
I stroll into the club,
when Sammy gets booed off the stage,
because of a joke he played that backfired.
"Show's over," the manager tells
the assortment of losers and swells,
so Sammy sits down at the bar.
I offer him a Cuban cigar,
then I light up another.
We smoke in silence,
broken only by the shush
of cars through the slush
of November, turning to winter.
"Ain't it a bitch," Sammy says, at last,
pitching ash in his whiskey,
which he drinks anyway.
"They killed the president
and it's like nothing happened."
I nod, I tug at my threadbare shirt,
as if it can protect me
from the infinite cold.
"One more for the road, babe?" he asks.
I say, no, one last toast
to the President, before I go,
then I raise my glass,
open my mouth wide and swallow.

MIRACLE IN MANILA

A man could never do
as much for Imelda
as a pair of shoes.
I always knew if she had to choose,
it would be pumps instead of passion.
Although her Ferdinand was handy
with his tongue and his fingers,
she preferred to linger
over coffee and a stack of magazines
rather than to have him between her legs.
I could only get the flower
of the Philippines in bed,
when I was dressed in a red jock strap
and tap shoes.
Even then, she might fade
into another rambling monologue,
or nap fitfully,
until I tap-danced and sang, "Feelings,"
a song I hated,
but marriage is a compromise
and many times, I had to sing two choruses,
before she woke and sang along
and with the last ounce of my energy,
I would take off those goddamn shoes
and do my duty as a man.
A woman like Imelda

must be wooed again and again,
because she is controlled by her moods,
which are dark and greedy,
and every day, they chew her up
and spit her out,
less a few clothes and jewels
and more of the slum she came from.
Now she's too old to play the ingenue.
The loyal few won't admit
that she no longer matters.
They grovel at her feet,
while she holds court
in a hotel suite.
Otherwise, she's mostly ignored,
so isolated and bored with herself,
she takes to her beloved stores.
She gives away her shopping bags of evening clothes
to the poor maids,
who have no more use for them than I do,
lying in my refrigerated coffin.
Finally, she has a meeting with Mother B,
who has been crucified every Good Friday
for the last five years.
Between sips of diet soda and tears,
Imelda decides the time is right
for her own brief sojourn on the cross,
so she goes to San Fernando with her entourage.
She wears a simple shift designed in Paris,
and handmade flats.
She even holds the special nails,
soaked in alcohol for a year,
to her nose, and inhales,

before she lets the attendants
drive them into her hands and feet,
just missing bones and blood vessels.
Only a few heartbeats and she is down,
waving to the crowd,
who shout her name,
as if she really is the president.
It's then she starts to bleed
from her palms.
Somebody screams, then they all do.
It seems like hours
before they rush toward her,
tearing at her clothes, her hair,
pleading for cures, for food,
for everything they've ever needed.
Only gunfire drives them back
and she flees, both horrified and pleased
that the trick worked.
Once the fake blood's washed off,
she stares at her hands,
almost wishing she really had stigmata.
She doesn't even make the news.
I mean, they get her confused with Mother B,
who seizes credit for the "miracle."
Imelda lets it go.
She settles for self-mockery
and sings "Memories,"
while her guests dine on Kentucky Fried Chicken,
flown in by Federal Express.
When she's alone, she gets undressed
and lies down,
not even bothering to get beneath the covers.

Next morning, they find her
drained of her blood,
but her heart's still beating
and she suddenly sits up,
repeating my name.
She says in a vision,
I gave her a pair of magic slippers,
that allow her to walk on water.
She's lying, but I'm past caring
and I'm done with shoes.
Anyway, she doesn't need me,
because she's got her illusions.
After a transfusion, a facial,
and a manicure,
she's campaigning again, although it's useless
and I'm back tap-dancing by her side,
while she proclaims herself
the only candidate
who can rise from the dead.

FINISHED

You force me to touch
the black, rubber flaps
of the garbage disposal
that is open like a mouth saying, ah.
You tell me it's the last thing I'll feel
before I go numb.
Is it my screaming that finally stops you,
or is it the fear
that even you are too near the edge
of this Niagara to come back from?
You jerk my hand out
and give me just enough room
to stagger around you.
I lean against the refrigerator,
not looking at you, or anything,
just staring at a space which you no longer inhabit,
that you've abandoned completely now
to footsteps receding
to the next feeding station,
where a woman will be eaten alive
after cocktails at five.
The flowers and chocolates, the kisses,
the swings and near misses of new love
will confuse her,
until you start to abuse her,
verbally at first.
As if trying to quench a thirst,

you'll drink her
in small outbursts of rage
then you'll whip out your semiautomatic,
make her undress, or listen to hours
of radio static as torture
for being amazed that the man of her dreams
is a nightmare, who only seems happy
when he's making her suffer.

The first time you hit me,
I left you, remember?
It was December. An icy rain was falling
and it froze on the roads,
so that driving was unsafe, but not as unsafe
as staying with you.
I ran outside in my nightgown,
while you yelled at me to come back.
When you came after me,
I was locked in the car.
You smashed the window with a crowbar,
but I drove off anyway.
I was back the next day
and we were on the bare mattress,
because you'd ripped up the sheets,
saying you'd teach me a lesson.
You wouldn't speak except
to tell me I needed discipline,
needed training in the fine art
of remaining still
when your fist slammed into my jaw.
You taught me how ropes could be tied
so I'd strangle myself,

how pressure could be applied to old wounds
until I cried for mercy,
until tonight, when those years
of our double exposure end
with shot after shot.

How strange it is to be unafraid.
When the police come,
I'm sitting at the table,
the cup of coffee
that I am unable to drink
as cold as your body.
I shot him, I say, he beat me.
I do not tell them how the emancipation from pain
leaves nothing in its place.

LIFE STORY

for Father Ritter and other priests accused of sexual abuse

Nuns are the brides of Christ,
but priests are His sons,
sons denied the sexual release
of giving themselves up to the spirit.
Christ is not raped, until he hails Caesar,
no, not Him,
but isn't it logical,
can't we imagine it going that far?
For examined in that context,
the rest snaps into place.
To rape is to erase the other's identity
and replace it with your own,
so why not ram it home, eh,
the Roman way (copied from the Greeks, of course).
Strip Him, whip Him, bend Him over and . . .
Suddenly, I imagine the blond hustler
with the black Georgia O'Keefe crosses
tattooed on his butt cheeks.
Ah, let me count the ways.
But most days, I conduct myself
in a conventional fashion.
I perform my desperate acts only in my thoughts.
I talk to God from one side of my mouth.
I say Mass, pass out the host
and most of the time,
I only drink wine for consolation,
but once in a while,

I raise the black flag of moral surrender
and I get out my visual aids.
My hand trembles, as I turn each page,
where men and boys are displayed like offerings,
their cocks to be seized and squeezed,
until I drown in jizzum,
until I leave my prison
to walk the tightrope
to the next broken boy,
the next indiscretion that could destroy me.
This one's what they used to call consumptive.
"Do you need a place to stay?" I ask.
In bed, he says, he's afraid of the dark,
so I leave the light on.
Toward daylight, I strike.
He says, "Daddy, don't,"
but daddy do and do
and when I'm through,
I give him a few dollars
and a card that says
Need Help? Call 1 (800) 4-Refuge.
But what about my own help line to salvation?
The voice always says,
I'm not in right now, leave a message,
so at the sound of sizzling flesh,
I repeat my request for rescue.
What is it I want to escape?
Are the boys merely substitutes
to save me from some greater abomination?
In my dreams, the centurion has my face,
holds Christ by the waist
and kisses his navel,

sticks his tongue there,
surprised to find the taste
of honey filling his mouth.
The sound of bees also fill his ears,
as he spreads his cloak on the floor
and shoves Christ down on it.
When he feels stinging in his groin,
he finds his pubic hair alive with bees.
His cock swells to an enormous size,
turns black and he dies,
staring into Christ's eyes.
Still He had not spoken,
had seemed to open and open Himself
to the centurion,
only to take His revenge
at the moment of consummation.
Am I going somewhere with this,
or am I only trying to discover who is who
in the locked room of sexual abuse?
One is the picture
and the other is the frame around it.
I found it!—the photograph
of Father Harrigan and me when I am five.
He holds me in his lap.
I'm tired, though I've had my nap.
It's June, I mean he said he had a june bug,
to come to his room to see.
Did I say he is my uncle?
By the time I'm thirteen,
we have so many secrets between us—
my tiny hand, a penis
that I stroke

the way he taught me,
he who bought me my first missal
and who later welcomes me into the seminary.
He teaches me how to capture little boys
with promises of toys,
until a free meal
becomes the lure
with which the fish
are hooked, then filleted
and cooked.
I remember how he shook me,
when I wouldn't touch.
"Do not tease me, boy. Please me," he said,
"or, or . . ."
He shuddered, he jerked away from me
and that was that, until next time.
Finally, I'm at his grave.
When I fall on my knees, father pulls me up.
"I know everything," he whispers, "I know.
When we get home, you pack. You leave."
When he has his final heart attack,
I sit with his body for hours.
I think some power to change
may drain from him to me,
but I feel nothing
brushing against my soul,
except the old urge.

After the funeral,
mother and I find letters from my uncle
in a tattered, old suitcase.
Before I can stop her, she opens them.

She smothers a cry
when she comes to the photograph of me
in the buff, a dust broom
stuck up my anus.
I stare at it, amazed I had forgotten it happened.
Uncle begs forgiveness, in each letter,
but father never forgives.
The last, dated the year before he died
is five pages (the shortest).
Again he describes how he robbed me of my innocence,
but says I can at least do good as a priest.
Twice mother tries to speak.
At last, she says, "You were always such a sweet boy."
She rips the letters up
and throws them in the trash.
"And give me that," she cries.
Finally, the photograph in shreds, she opens her hands
in a gesture of helplessness,
then says, "I'll fix you supper."

Later, we embrace and I go outside.
I spread my arms around the ancient oak,
where uncle tied me once,
until I took him inside my mouth.
I thought my throat would close,
but instead it froze open,
while snow and semen
spilled down into me.
I was ten and I was praying to die,
praying I would choke,
while he commanded me to open wider.
Finally, I couldn't breathe.

I passed out and when I came 'round,
my mouth tasted of soap.
Uncle spoke, "Lie on your side."
I felt him poking me with something,
then I felt myself pried apart,
as I began to lose consciousness again.
"Still friends?" he asked next time.
"What are you drawing?"
It was a flying man, his head
severed from his body
and falling to earth,
but I said, "It's the Holy Ghost."
"No," he said, "this is your uncle,
this is the end of hope."
He hung himself with rope.
We priests did our best to hide it,
pretended not to know the truth,
though the proof was in his room.
One filthy magazine after another
and nude photos, scattered on the bed and floor
were there for unavoidable discovery.
They delegated me the burning
of the evidence,
the lies about the whys of his closed casket.
We found a way around it all,
got him into hallowed ground.
An accident, a fall, we told everyone.
Hit his head, bled profusely,
found dead hours later . . .
I slammed his head against the radiator,
then notified the police.
We came to an agreement

for the good of the Church.
They would not release the report.
We could sort it out ourselves, couldn't we?

I throw my duffle in the car
and back out of the drive.
When the hustler I pick up
moves across the seat,
I feel no beast rising beneath his hand.
"Go on, get out," I say
"and stay away from creeps like me."
"I'll see you again," he says, because he knows.
I know he will too, unless I lose my head some afternoon
and like a June bride, marry groom death.
At the next intersection,
I head west, instead of south.
Along the way, I shed my priesthood
like a skin.
I work my way from one end
of decline to another.
Sometimes I drink for days,
then take any job that pays enough
for sandwiches.
After two thousand miles, I sell the car
and tend bar in Wickenburg,
until a memory disturbs my false serenity.
Twin boys, who lived on our street,
forced to eat off the floor,
while uncle bored into them
with a vibrator.
Later, he showed a video of Peter Pan,
which was written by a man

not too different from me,
for as I understand it,
Captain Hook may be taken
as the unexpressed desire
to molest a child, to threaten him with harm,
then ultimately to defile him.
Now when people stare at the stub
where my hand was, I smile and rub it,
as if a genie will appear
and grant three wishes.
I am that which I fear.
Is that why you cleared out, uncle dear,
though here you are in a puff of smoke,
the scar of your life healed over now.
How much farther must I go?
Why is my destination so uncertain?
What is the difference between nothing and zero?
Cackling, you fade to black
and I'm staring through the bars
at L.A. County, where I am incarcerated
for another sex-related incident
that escalated into violence.
He participated willingly I told them,
as the boy was hustled off
to join the war against the saints,
who aren't just the good ones, no,
but also the ones who struggle again and again
against the flow of raw sewage,
only to drown in its undertow.

PENIS ENVY

My wife deserved to be shot.
I served time in the Gulf,
and I am telling you
when I came home and found her packed up and gone,
it wasn't long until I hatched a plan.
I located the man behind it all,
staked out his apartment and his job.
Then one afternoon, I dressed up in camouflage,
loaded my AK-47
and went to Hot Dog Heaven.
I found them in the parking lot,
sharing kisses over lunch.
I came up from behind, but changed my mind
and walked right in front,
and aimed through the windshield,
before they had a chance to see who it was.
I shouted my name, hoping she would hear as she died,
then I went to the passenger side
and fired at his head. A red mass
exploded like a sunburst.
At first, I couldn't believe I'd done it,
then I put the gun down
and looked at my hands, which were steady.
I pulled open the door,
before I knew what I was doing.

I just had to see what he was hiding in his pants.
It was pathetic, a sad, shriveled thing
there between his legs
and not the foot-long
she had said made her scream with pleasure.
I did hear screams, but they were coming
from my mouth, not hers.
Noise, I thought, as I fired at her body again.
Of course, I'd turned the gun on myself.
What else could I do to erase it all?—
the 911 calls, the sirens in the distance,
but the ordinariness of murder overwhelmed me,
possessed me like a spirit
and I thought how easy it would be
to take two or three more people with me.
Instead, I decided to give myself up,
plus I was out of ammunition.
I guess it is my destiny,
to be a living example for other men,
who are only bluffing when they threaten violence.
Now once a week, I write a column on relationships
for the prison publication.
I base my advice on actual situations.
For example, Clarence Thomas.
He had a dick fixation, just as I did.
For me, it was a torment and my downfall
and nearly his.
Ultimately, the question is always
how far are you willing to go?
I think within his parameters,

Clarence went the distance.
As far as I'm concerned,
he's earned his place on the Supreme Court
and stands tall beside all the other men,
who haven't given in to a woman's scorn,
who are born again from the fire of their ridicule.
If you ask me, Anita Hill got off too easily.
I would have caught the bitch
some afternoon, while the cherry blossoms
were in bloom
and boom, solved all my problems.
Oops! I think I wobbled over the line
that separates fantasy from crime.
The counselors tell me all the time
I've got to get it straight
how the imagination sometimes
races on without us.
But I know Debby and Ed are off somewhere
eating wedding cake
and letting me take the fall for their betrayal.
Is it fair that on the other side of this wall
Clarence has it all
and I have nothing but a ball and chain?
That reminds me, I checked this Othello play
out of the library.
It's about a guy
who loses his reputation and his wife,
well, he kills her, but she made him.
I found some parallels to my own life and Clarence's.
Othello's black.
But the other subtler thing is how a man

must stand up to humiliation,
must retaliate, or lose himself,
who when he finds some pubic hair
in his can of Coke
must ask, regardless of the consequences,
who put it there?

GREED

I was named after my daddy, Vern,
but I was like my mama,
though I'd never admit it, until now.
Before she settled down,
she traveled from town to town
on the roller derby circuit
for the Texas Tornadoes.
Sometimes I went with her.
She always knew how to make me happy.
She'd take me to the nearest hot dog stand
and tell the man,
"Give Verna the works."
She was a big-boned farm girl with flame-red hair
and with the smallest, most delicate feet.
She had to have her skates made specially
and even then, she had to fill them in
with wads of cotton.
I looked like her, but I had daddy's feet,
wide, flat, and reliable.
I wore cowboy boots, a cowboy hat and jeans,
and I was high school rodeo queen of '75.
I learned to drive a tractor, brand cattle
and spit, after I took a bit of chaw.
The boys admired me and asked me out,
but I didn't trust them. They talked too much,
but Russ, the Viet Nam vet,
who drove the school bus was fine for me,

though all in all I'd have to say I wasn't half the girl
I could have been.
A wild mother sometimes makes a cautious child,
who takes the safest path to her destination.
In my case, it was a savings and loan bank,
where at nineteen, I sank
into the routine of being secretary
to Mr. Joe Bob Merriweather,
the president and decent, churchgoing family man.

My change of life began in '82,
when money started pouring in here
like heavy rain through a leaky roof.
All we had to do was set out buckets anyplace
and we would catch a mess of money.
I was polishing my nails lunch time one day,
when a man sailed in the door
and asked me for a date.
Just then, Joe Bob came out
and without a glance at me said, "Boy, she's taken."
After that, we were making love
at least three times a week,
sometimes across the desk
or in the backseat of his Pontiac.
He wasn't that good at it,
but he tried and I was grateful
just to be at his side,
when all his deals paid off.
Then he bought a Rolls.
He partied with politicians and whores,
until word got back to his wife

and she threatened to slit off a piece
of you know what.
After that, he thought he'd better quit it with me too,
so he bought me a sable coat from SAKS JANDEL.
He wished me well
and I sat at my desk, reading the *Wall Street Journal*.
I dabbled in real estate with my latest raise.
I was making one hundred thousand dollars a year,
plus monthly bonus,
and Joe Bob was clearing millions,
building condos, financed through his S & L,
his own contractors, and just plain old-fashioned kickbacks.
We were riding the crest of deregulations wave.
The S & L was like a building without foundation.
How could it stand
longer than a man's imagination?
We were drowning in the illusion of money.
We couldn't be saved.
But that was later.
For a while, I slaved for him,
but then I thought I'd work for my own benefit.
I told mama how he'd used me like I was a slut
he could tip when he got done.
All she said was, "You're just like me.
I could skate all right,
but I couldn't pick men worth a damn.
Your father's a fine example.
You have the brains, the looks.
What took you so long to get what you want?"
I told Joe Bob I'd tell his wife about us.
I said, "Pleading won't get you anywhere.
You're a betting man.

Take out the cards
and deal this hand."
When I went in my own office at last, I cried,
then poured a glass of champagne,
opened a box of Godiva chocolates,
and put my feet up on the desk.
The rest of the time, I learned the trade.
I stayed out of Joe Bob's way and he out of mine.
In time, I had my clients too, a few deals
that added up to two million dollars
in my personal account,
but you know, it didn't amount to much
without love,
which I didn't know was coming
in the form of Bubba Taylor.
Yes, love and hate were waiting in his arms.
He was a charming scoundrel,
who found a way to get my money
that was just setting like a laying hen on eggs.
When he got between my legs,
I was begging for destruction
and it came a mere six months to the day
after I met him.
He robbed me is what he did.
I admit I gave him access to my accounts.
He was my fiancé, wasn't he?
He disappeared just like he'd come
and I had to start over,
only now the government was cracking down
on what it once had ballyhooed
as the way to turn around the banking industry
and free it from the controls

it had enacted in the first place.
Ronald Reagan and his bunch threw out the rules,
but did not go down on the ship of fools,
when it foundered. We did
and we took a lot of people with us.
The unsold real estate piled up—
apartment buildings, condos, homes, and office towers.
Loans in default.
We ought to have known it couldn't last,
but we were past all reasoning.
We had to keep the money moving back and forth
to cover up the fact
that Santa Claus's sack was empty.

Joe Bob took off for parts unknown
and I went home to Abilene,
but not for long.
I was called back to Dallas to testify.
Joe Bob was tried and sentenced to twenty-five years
minimum security, reduced to three,
and when I finished my spiral down
the chain of lies,
I took up keeping books
at Clem's West Side Auto Supply.
They claim the S & L's are getting bailed out,
though it sounds like some of the same shenanigans
are going on at RTC.
They're moving money into other bottomless pockets,
behind the screen of fixing things.
The whole country's on the edge of insolvency,
but I am watching from the sidelines now
like a drunk who's pledged to stay off the bottle,

but the ledge where I'm standing is so narrow.
I could fall back in the fire,
where the money's burning like desire,
only with much more intensity.
Finally, mama and me moved to Vegas,
where I cocktail-waitress at the Sands
and each paycheck I tell the man
at the craps table,
let it ride, until it hurts.

NEW POEMS

RAPTURE

A Fiction

Memory is a highway,
where a car is speeding into the sunset.
The man inside that car has a gun.
He says he'll shoot himself
and be done with it, be dead,
but in the end, he doesn't do it.
If he had, the path to the truth
would have led straight from the gate
outside his ex-wife's house,
not end run around it,
leaving a trail of blood
the prosecution says is proof
that he used his power, his juice
to seduce death
by handing her two sacrifices,
but she promised what she would never deliver.
She left him a pair of loaded dice
and severed their connection
with one well-practiced slice.

Now in his cell,
he reads fan letters.
He doesn't dwell on the past.
If he did, he'd tell you to always go for broke,
because a man who can't go the distance is a joke,
is a failure.
"You can quote me on that," he says aloud,

then shocked by the sound of his own voice,
chokes back a cry.
When he looks himself in the eye,
he just sees a regular guy.
He sees a parade going by.
On the largest float,
the homecoming queen waves to the crowd.
She's a statuesque blond.
He's a football hero.
He's also a black man,
but that is no obstacle.
It's a license to do the impossible.
He waves back.
Maybe that isn't really what happened,
but it's close and he makes the most of it,
when he can see through the smoke
of his desire and his rage.
In a flash,
he feels the diamonds of hope,
cutting the smooth glass of his mind
into halfs and quarters,
as he runs backward in time,
a football tucked under his arm,
as he crosses the goal line,
only to find the stands are empty
and he is alone on the field.
Concealed in the ball is a bomb.
All he has to do to explode it is throw.
He listens to the silence inhaling,
then he lets go.
That's when the crowd appears
and over the loudspeaker

he hears his coach, saying, "Buddy, come on home,"
but home is the scene of the crime,
shown on TV so many times
that the murderer and victims cease to exist,
except in peripheral vision
and in the void between the goalposts,
thirty-two bits and pieces of his life
are all that survive the knife.

FALSE WITNESS

A Fiction

I did not buy you the tiara
with the fake jewels,
because your father said it made you look cheap,
although eventually, he confessed
that he was thrilled
to think of you wearing only tap shoes
and your crown of silver plate and paste,
but you took it out on me, you vixen.
That's when I swore to myself that you'd regret
making me get on my knees
and beg your forgiveness,
so you would play with Daddy
the way I taught you.
While I kneeled,
you told me I was a bad mommy
and made a face at me.
After I apologized,
I cut a crude tiara from cardboard
and set it on your head.
I said, "I'll buy you a real one tomorrow."
"But tomorrow's Christmas," you cried.
"The store will be open," I lied.
You knew it, but decided to taunt your father
instead of arguing with me.
You called him a mean old daddy
and pinched him hard,

then you played hide-and-seek
under the goose-down comforter,
until I said, "game."
Later, he told me he didn't know a six year old
could be such a cruel mistress
and I said, "Making men suffer is her destiny."
I was his enemy and you were my collaborator.
At first, I didn't even want you to be as debauched
as I had been, when my father first came to my bed,
but instead of suffering, you thrived
and so did your father,
or am I lying to myself to ease my guilt?
Lately, it lies back of my mind like silt
that I sift through
to try to find the woman
who became a mother
with no other thought than of revenge.
When you were five,
I tutored you in the art of seduction.
"Sit on Daddy's lap and rub your back against him," I said.
"Squirm too and don't be afraid of the bulge there.
It's made for girls like you."
And girls like me,
although sometimes I think that nothing happened
when my father said good night,
that he simply shut off the light
and closed the door
and I am an unreliable witness to my own life,
but if I'm not, I'm warning you
I won't be a victim twice.
You have too much power over your father now

and through him, over me.
Last evening, when I asked you to say grace,
you even stood up and showed me your panties
with the red hearts on them,
the ones I gave you after your first time.
Now you give your father a grudging kiss
that has no passion in it,
no tongue that tastes like a strawberry lollipop.
Although he pleads with you,
you keep your lips pressed together.
I tell him to let it go,
but he says the memory of that taste inflames him.
He says it's as though he's lying in a bowl
of strawberries and cream,
waiting to be devoured.
As I unbutton your pajama top,
he buries his face in the nest of your golden hair.
As usual, he starts to cry.
You are unmoved.
You sigh and reach for your favorite doll,
but I take her and throw her on the floor.
I think I see the glint of your father's tears
on your skin,
as I get the rope
and put it around your neck,
then I take the stick, insert it and twist.
"This is how to satisfy her," I tell him.
"Why do you make me suffer," he whimpers,
"because you know you can?"
Your mouth is half open,
as if you are about to speak.
I stare at you, looking for a sign

that you and I are kin,
but you are an imitation of the diamond that I am.
See what happens to naughty little girls?
They pay for their disobedience
in the arms of their fathers
at childhood's end.

SLEEPING BEAUTY

A Fiction

for the comatose patient raped by an aide

You steal into my room,
between darkness and noon
to doff the disguise as nurse's aide
and parade before me as you really are,
a man for whom time is deranged
and consists of your furtive visits to me,
while all the rest is just a gloomy reprieve
from your nothingness.
For me time is arranged without the past
or the future,
without tenses to suture me to my days and nights.
For me, there is only now,
when you are certain you won't be disturbed,
spread my legs apart
and break through the red door to my chamber.
After you've finished,
you use a clean, white towel
to wipe away the evidence
of how you mingled your life
with what is left of mine.
You think your crime won't be discovered
but the evidence survives
to dine on the flow of fluid
dripping into me,
as though I were merely a conduit

for the baby who knows me
only as its host
and never will as Mother
and you will never be Father,
baby never see,
you, who in a fever came to me.
I was "comma tose" as my mother calls it.
She hoped for a miracle,
but when it came, it was not the one she wanted,
when she prayed to Saint Jude,
patron saint of lost causes
and laid my photo on the altar
she'd erected in the living room,
beside a rose in a crystal vase.
My face almost glowed in the dark,
as if the spark of consciousness
leaped from me into the image
of what I was before I was swept away from myself,
only to return as someone else,
for whom language is silence,
language is thirst
that is not slaked.
Monster, you took all that was left of my body,
but could not break my body's vow
of renunciation of itself.
My eyes were open,
while you violated me.
All at once
you raised your hand and closed them,
but I could see
beyond the veil of your deceit.
At first, I thought you'd come to my rescue,

but instead of waking me with a kiss,
you pricked me with the thorn of violence
and I did not rise from by bed
to wed the handsome prince
as in the fairy tale
my mother once read to me,
when *forever* did not mean eternity.

CHARISMA

A Fiction

I didn't just read the Bible, I lived it.
I told my people, this is revolution.
I said, I interpret this attack
on my constitutional rights
with a gun and a guitar
to mean we are in trouble.
I held up a hand grenade, pulled the pin
and told them, "This one's for Jesus."
I prayed, "Lord, take me to heaven, take me today
and I won't falter on the way."
Did my people desert me,
did they say this man is crazy?
No, they didn't.
They prayed with me.
They lay facedown in Waco, Texas,
to await death and resurrection,
as it came from all directions, all in flames.
I never claimed to be the Jesus, who cured the sick
and caused the lame to walk.
I knew the sins of the flesh, I knew the shame
and I confessed my weakness.
I let my people be witness to it
and through it came my power
and the empty talk of changing sinful ways
that haunt a man,
until he betrays himself no longer
and gives in to the stronger urge

to fornicate and multiply dissolved.
I absolved myself between a woman's thighs
and I arose like Lazarus,
raised up from the dead
on the tip of his penis.
We had no life and death between us anymore,
we had rounds of ammunition
and all of you to listen to us burn
and in that burning learn
how to give your life for freedom
in Christian hunting season.
The AFT used child abuse as the excuse
to assault us in our home.
They had no proof
and if we had been left alone,
we might have shown the world
that God is like desire you cannot satisfy.
You must give in to Him, or die.
The Apocalypse cometh like a firestorm,
leaving some of us reborn,
others to smolder in the ruins
of New Jerusalem,
which will not come again,
until the war against the innocent is over.

THE ANTIHERO

A Fiction

for Police Officer Terry Yeakey, who committed suicide four days before he was to receive a medal of honor for rescuing people after the Oklahoma City bombing

I park my old maroon Ford in the field outside El Reno,
where wildflowers used to grow, when I was a kid,
but now only thorny memories push their heads
through the dirt like misplaced cacti.
At first, I just sit in the dark,
my heart racing,
then I take my Swiss Army Knife
and slit my wrists.
As blood runs down my hands, I feel exhilerated,
until I remember who I am—
a man with rat's eyes,
pink rimmed and sensitive to light.
When I was born,
the doctor pronounced me "albino."
I'm told my mother said,
"They run in the family,
but he's all right, he's my baby."
Six months later, I was adopted by another,
who loved me even though I wasn't an albino after all.
Much like a Siamese, who are born white,
parts of my body began to darken,
until I looked like any other boy.
When I was nine, Widow Dobbs, who lived next door,

brought home a Siamese.
She named him Buster Kitty.
He was a big, round-headed cat,
who hunted birds and tormented dogs,
when he wasn't sitting outside my window,
looking in at me,
as if I were a long-lost relative.
We respected each other,
but avoided too much contact.
When I went outside to play, he'd stroll away,
his tail lifted in the air, as if to say, "Take that."
One afternoon, he got run over by a moving van.
Widow Dobbs wasn't home and neither was my mother,
so I carried him to our backyard
and buried him in a hole I dug with a garden trowel.
I didn't tell anyone I'd done it.
After a week, the widow put up signs
offering a reward.
A few months later,
a stray dog dug up Buster's skeleton.
"I suppose you know nothing about it," said Mother.
"A truck hit him, he was dead, so I buried him," I confessed,
but Mother only said, "I found your water pistol."
Now Buster sits on my shoulder,
whispering that I'll get what I deserve.
I tell him I always do.
I used to see him two, or three times a day,
when I was a military policeman,
during the Persian Gulf War.
That's when I helped bury civilians in mass graves.
The corpses gave off the smell of chemicals and oil

and when I washed my hands,
a black film came off on my Handi Wipes.
There, as the smoke from the burning oil wells
blackened the light of each day,
I picked up the carcasses of birds
overcome by fumes,
having dropped from the air
after dying in midflight.
I buried them too,
as Buster scolded me about how I placed the bodies.
"No," he'd say, "don't drop them in like stones
down the well of death,"
and I didn't. I laid them down gently
like a mother, who has found her lost children.
After a while, he simply faded
into the scenery of that endless night
and when I went home to Oklahoma City,
he kept his distance.
It was enough to convince me that I was free of him,
until the day the Murrah building was bombed.
I was a policeman then too,
because I'd persuaded myself
it was the best way to help people.
That morning, I pulled three men and two women
from the rubble,
before I fell through a hole two floors
and lay helpless in the debris.
As body fluids dripped on me, Buster appeared,
but he didn't say anything,
only hovered in the air, until I passed out.
After I came home from the hospital,

my back hurt constantly
and I had nightmares about dead children.
I was afraid of what I might do,
without knowing what it was.
Waves of nausea often sent me to the bathroom,
where I kneeled in front of the toilet,
until a vile liquid bubbled up
from the pit of my stomach.
It tasted like green chilies
and burned the back of my throat.
I pissed blood and cursed Buster,
who truly knew me for what I was,
because I was to blame for his death
and hid my shame by covering it with dirt.
The day he died, I shot him with my water pistol.
That's when he darted in the path
of a Bekins truck.
That night, I made a promise to myself
that I would be of help to anyone who needed it.
Now as I listen to the drip, drip of my blood,
hitting the rubber floor mat and my shoes,
I realize I can't rescue the dead,
or erase the zero of my life
and make it count,
when all it amounts to is a few pints of blood,
turning to red mud,
as I stagger from the car to a gully nearby.
I kneel down and lay my Bible
and copy of *In Their Names* on the ground,
as Buster reappears to tell me it's all right,
I won't feel a thing,

but we both know he's lying
and when I raise my revolver to my head and fire,
a wave of desire washes over me
and I understand that what I always wanted
was release from my own pain,
but there's only the terrible surrender to it.

RWANDA

My neighbor used to come to our hut,
bringing melons so sweet
I thought I should not eat them,
because I would die
and haunt my family like a ghost
with hard, black seeds for eyes.
One day, he brought his uncle and two friends
and they asked my father to go outside with them.
I thought he had come to get permission to marry me
and I was glad because I loved him,
even though he wasn't a member of my tribe,
nor as educated as I was.
I wanted to stay,
but my mother gave me a basket of clothes
to wash at the river.
She said, "Don't come back,
until they are as clean as the Virgin Mary's soul."
"Mother," I said, "I'll never come back then."
"Shall I take my brother?" I asked,
as he ran to my father's side.
I was laughing, when she hissed, "Run,"
and I did because she frightened me.
As I rounded the hut,
I heard the *tat, tat, tat,* from guns
like the ones the soldiers carry.
I ran faster, still holding the basket.
It was frozen to my hands

and I still held it, even as I jumped in the river.
I thought I would die, so I closed my eyes.
When something bumped against me,
I opened them and saw my father's body.
As he floated past me,
his arm hooked around my neck,
almost taking me under
and I released the basket.
I reached for my father, as bullets hit the water
and I dove under him.
His body shielded me, until I couldn't breathe
and had to break the surface for air.
When I crawled onto the riverbank,
I hid in the grass behind the church.
Finally, when I was sure no one was around,
I beat on the rectory door,
until the priest opened it. "Hide me, Father," I begged.
Once inside, I was overjoyed to see my mother.
She told me when my neighbor shot at her,
she pretended to be dead
and while he dumped my father in the river,
she escaped and came here,
hoping I had survived.
She said we needed another place to hide,
but she could only find a small closet-size space
behind the altar, covered by a sheet of tin.
Only one of us could fit, so she made me go in
and covered the hole again.
When I heard screaming, I kicked the tin aside
and saw my mother was on fire.
I tried to help her, using only my hands,
but when she was completely covered in flames,

I broke a stained-glass window
with a statue of Saint Joseph and climbed out.
As I crawled back to the river,
a shiver of wind passed over me
through the grass and trees.
When I stopped to rest,
fear coiled around me like a snake,
but when I told myself I would not let them kill me,
it took the shape of a bird and flew away.
I crawled back to the church,
because I wanted to find my mother's ashes,
so I could bury them,
but my way was blocked by the rebels,
so I waited until dark.
Maybe I slept. I don't know.
When I heard my neighbor's voice,
it was as if I had awakened from a dream.
Relief flooded over me, until I sat up
and saw him standing above me, holding a machete.
"Sister," he said, "I won't hurt you."
I knew he was lying and I tried to get away,
but I was too weak
and he fell on top of me, tearing at my clothes.
When he was finished raping me,
I thought he would kill me,
but he only brought the machete close to my head,
then let it fall from his hands.
Dawn had come to the village
with more killing on its mind.
I heard screams and pleas for mercy,
then I realized those sounds were inside me.
They would never leave.

Now I am always talking to the dead.
Their bones are rattling around in my head.
Sometimes I can't hear anything else
and I go to the river with my son and cry.
When he was a few days old,
I took him there for the first time.
I stood looking at the water,
which was still the color of blood,
then I lifted him high above my head,
but my mother's bones said, "Killing is a sin,"
so I took him home
to raise him as if he really is my son
and not the issue of my neighbor,
who has returned to torment me
with skin that smells like burning flesh,
but in my heart I know
both his mother and father died long ago
and left this orphan to grow like a poisoned flower
beside the open grave that was my country.

STALKING MEMORY

Three months ago, I stabbed your cactus plant.
I thought that would be the end of it,
until I decided if I couldn't steal your heart,
I'd steal your peace of mind.
While you were gone today,
I broke into your house.
I rifled through your underwear drawer.
I held your panties to my nose
to inhale the scent of you,
but as I closed my eyes,
all I smelled was the odor of bleach.
One day soon,
when you've been seized by fear
as I have by love, my dear,
you'll be as bound as I am freed
from all restraints, except need.
I want to make you understand
how that need grew and grew,
until it consumed me.
I want to teach you what it's like
to live your life for someone else
with no regard for self.
Only you matter,
you whose throat I'd like to tear open
with my teeth, but I'm no werewolf,
I'm simply part of this ordinary night,

when you turn out the light and sleep,
unaware that I am sliding under the sheet
to lie beside you.
I'm so sorry I have to gag you and tie you up.
It isn't part of the plan,
but neither is my hand
inside the waistband of your pajama bottoms.
I only intend to beg you to kill me
and end my agony,
but suddenly, I see the past,
the present, and the future
all shouting at me like giant mouths
to "Do it, do it,"
and when you bite through the flimsy scarf
and try to scream,
I have to take extreme measures.
At first, I don't know how I'll live without you,
but after I get dressed, I'm sure I will.

Outside, the early morning air chills me
and I'm glad I brought a sweater.
Underneath your welcome mat,
I find my last letter to you.
I feel so much better now
that I don't have to wait for you to read it.
From now on, I resolve to be the kind of person
you would have wanted,
so I water all your plants, before I leave.
Once, I stood outside your bedroom window
barely breathing in the dark

and just two nights ago, parked my car
half a block away
and stayed awake by saying your name,
which after I shower, dress,
and go to work an hour early,
I'm afraid I can't remember.

THE PAPARAZZI

I'm on the ledge
outside your hotel bedroom,
when I glimpse your current lover,
as he bends over you on the bed
and deposits a cherry
he holds between his teeth
atop the mound of your very dark brown hair.
You're blonde to your adoring fans,
but I know where you're not.
For a second, I feel hot,
as I watch him, but I should be cold,
get the shot,
and go trespass on some other private property.
Come on baby, come.
I've got to pursue another asshole,
who thinks a TV role
makes him too good to be exposed warts and all
to those insatiable public coconspirators,
who want to know
all his dirty, little secrets,
or just his brand of soap.
The alcohol, miscarriages, divorces
marriages, face-lifts, coke binges,
homosexual, hetero and lesbian affairs.
I've been there through it all
and I am there for you,
a friend, not an enemy,

stalkerazzi, or a tabloid Nazi,
storm-trooping onto your yacht
to photograph you
in your latest embarrassing situation.
Think of me as a station of your cross
and the camera as your confessor,
who absolves you,
as you admit to lesser crimes
than I know you are guilty of.
You media whore, I didn't ask you for excuses,
I asked you for more
and I know you'll give it to me
before the public moves on
to the next shooting star,
but even then, occasionally I'll still
ambush you in rehab
and send the message
from the land of the fading career
that you are tumbling
through the stratosphere
just like you used to,
but now the only sound you hear
as you hit bottom once again
is the click of the shutter
and not applause and cheers.
I don't want the truth,
I want the lies,
so look this way,
say something nasty.
Don't be shy.

AFTERSCHOOL LESSONS FROM A HITMAN

What I do is
our secret.
Sh-h-h-h.
You gotta tell
I gotta bury it deep
deeper than that.
Everything is fine.
Everything is copacetic
as long as you keep
it all to yourself.
Don't let it—
Open your mouth.
Open it wider.

If you're gonna cry—

Your mother can't help.
Your father can't either.

A man is a man.
Sometimes he's neither.

You'll learn as you go.
You'll learn just like I did.

You know what you know.
You know kid?

That time in Jersey,
I put away my piece calmly
and eased past the customers,
looked straight ahead,
made it to the sidewalk,
got into the car
I left running.

You with me
so far?

U-m-m.

Now pull up your pants
and get outta my sight.

If I gotta dance,
I gotta dance solo
all right?

One more thing.
There's always a chance,
a chance that the hit might—
No, don't think about it.
Just go.

Wait. Take this calzone
my mother made
to your mother.

Hey, how's your brother?
Bring him next time.

You're never too young to
learn things.

I promise.
You'll know what I know.

I always say
it ain't a shame;
it's crime
and thank God somebody else
is paying.
This time.

CHANCE

written on learning of nuclear tests on unsuspecting civilians by the U.S. Government

An ill wind with a Samsonite suitcase
was passing through White Sands, New Mexico,
in February, 1952,
when Mama, Daddy, my little sister and I
were en route to Tucson
from Fort Riley, Kansas.
We were on a vacation
no one knew would take Daddy to the cancer ward.
The hard facts can't be taken back,
or rearranged like Scrabble pieces
to form another word that is not terminal.
"Open the windows," said Daddy.
"Let in some fresh air. Don't tell me
you girls have to use the bathroom again.
We'll stop when we see a gas station
and please, Stella,
don't take any towels, or soap.
We don't want to look bad being Negroes.
It won't be good for the race."
"They'll just say we stole anyway," said Mama,
as we drove through the gray afternoon.
The sand was as white as the dress of a bride.
The sky was a groom, pressing down on her.
Their union was doomed to disaster, but who knew,
as we pulled to a stop and Mama got out
and scooped up some sand

she planned to store with the other souvenirs
she bore home in triumph?
I had on my red Roy Rogers cowboy hat,
my western shirt, cowboy boots, and Levi's
and I pulled my cap gun from its holster and fired
at the dim outline of the sun,
as the wind blew up the highway
to the next defenseless, unsuspecting town.

The other day, I found a mirror
Mama appropriated so long ago
and when I looked in it,
I saw us in our old Ford
with one door held closed by chicken wire.
Back then, Daddy had faith in Jesus and democracy.
He didn't fear what he couldn't see, taste, or feel,
as he laid his hands on the steering wheel
and drove into his own nuclear winter.

KNOCK, KNOCK

A Fiction

"Do you want a silver bullet?"
           —Richard Nixon

Mother, help me. I feel as if I'm falling
from a great height,
as cold night sweats send me
shivering to the bathroom for fresh towels, more towels.
It feels as though it's ten below in here.
The heat is on,
but I'm cold and my footsteps
echo like a verdict,
spoken by an entire nation, "Guilty, guilty."
Now that Watergate's exploded like an atom bomb,
not even the Twenty-third Psalm can comfort me,
so I decide to drink another silver bullet.
When I turn on the air-conditioning,
because I want to hear the rumble of something
beside the artillery in my head,
when I lay it on the pillow
on the bed that might as well be a coffin,
I remember how comforting a fire is.
I take a few truly harmless scraps of paper
and add them to the wood in the fireplace
and I think, good, I am doing something practical.
Mother would be proud of me.
Mother, my cloud with the silver lining is a shroud
and I am dying without a shot being fired.

If Dick was going under, he wanted it to be
from a round of bullets,
because of some conspiracy he couldn't see coming,
when he was too busy running the country,
not because the men
who should have protected him let him down.
Isn't it pitiful that in the end,
all he had was slim chance, then none?
When other men could walk, I had to run.
I always had to be the one playing catch-up,
so I eavesdropped outside the doors of power
and before I stepped inside,
I knew the day, the hour and the score.
I am a sore loser, a sore winner
and what's more, I'm not ashamed of it.
The East Coast elite hate me,
because I'm poor.
They take me for an ass,
but I am a bull elephant,
rampaging through this cruel night,
before I take my final flight on *Air Force One*.
Mother, how come they all dislike Dick?
How come they spit, when he walks by
and when he looks them in the eyes, turn away?
Haven't I already paid a thousand times more
for my mistakes than any other president?
But if impeaching Dick is what it takes
to keep the country in the game,
then he says, "Go on, shake and bake him,
make him cry for mercy."
Mother, let's drink to new beginnings.
Let's celebrate my last night in office

with a toast to what is past,
then toss our glasses in the fireplace.
Stay with me. Please tell me what to do.
What's that, Mother?
You really think I should?
Yes, I agree, to go down in history
with a gesture says it best.
How about this one?
Of course, it's obscene.
Well, perhaps you're right.
It might offend somebody's mother.
Dick doesn't want that on his conscience.
"V" for victory then.
It's statesmanlike.
It's in good taste.
It's Dick.

BLOOD IN THE WATER

A Fiction

written after learning about a presidential affair

My grandaddy told me a man is nothing but appetite
sandwiched between his wife and mean lust.
I have a deep affection for my wife,
but also for the sweet, big-haired girls I'm partial to,
who never complain of tired jaws.
For a few stolen moments, I give them the deed to my heart,
signed and sealed with the only part of me
I've come to think is real.
At home, my wife telephones her friends
for advice about our marriage she never takes
and when I'm hot for her (not often)
makes me wait so long while she is in the bathroom
doing God knows what
I must take my own pleasure
and by the time she gets in bed,
I'm half asleep, my body depleted by the sheer effort
of keeping my desire for her alive.
We've been together well past the time
when couples find each other sexually attractive.
We have our child and our shared interests
which carry us forward each year,
without concern, or fear that one of us
will hear and heed the call of the wild
and seek permanent freedom in the arms of a warmer body.
No, there's comfort in a hot toddy

with an old friend beside the fire.
We're more like cousins,
who grew up together now
and when the feather of desire tickles us,
we smile and resume our separate lives
within the cocoon of malice, known as husband and wife,
having already experienced too much of kinship.
Doesn't everyone need to escape
from family business now and again?
Why then are my enemies and even some of my friends
beginning to shake their heads
and send me faxes about morality
and how the free love movement of the sixties
lead to these public and humiliating revelations
of my supposed liason with a young woman
I swear I do not know in the biblical sense,
although she presented herself to me
as if on a plate,
surrounded by French fries?
I saw in her eyes as she lay there
not submission to my will
but two hamburger patties sizzling on a grill.
They said, "Eat your fill,"
and God I wanted to, God, I willed myself
to refuse that generous offering
that now is being used
to justify the attempt by my rivals
to make me lose everything.
Now I stand as if naked on the evening news,
my chances of survival discussed
with no more care
than if I were dust,

beneath the heels of the righteous,
who are just as capable as I am
of falling from their high perches
into the muck that will suck them under
as it is doing me
once they are revealed to be human,
with human frailty.
My wife trusts me within the boundaries
we've set for each other;
yet the media and the other sharks,
who get off on seeing lives destroyed
won't accept that this is nothing
but another attempt to trap me in a lie.
Will a semen stain on a dress match my DNA?
Will I pay for my indiscretion? They ask,
as if it is a question that should be answered.
Damn them. Damn their eyes
and pass me the tortilla chips, salsa
and the latest polls,
so I can see what the public thinks of me.
They're not fooled.
They are forgiving
in spite of the jokes made at my expense
during monologues by TV hosts.
Although my rivals say if I'm not impeached
I'll lead the country into the twenty-first century
with my fly open, the electorate has spoken,
so subpoena me, subpoena everyone I know.
I am the captain of this ship of state
and I will sail us through the stormy seas of sleaze,
or we will all go down together
on our knees.

BACK IN THE WORLD

for Norman Fox

I took a shortcut through blood
to get back to you,
but the house where I left you is empty now.
You've packed up and moved on,
leaving this old photograph of the two of us,
taken before I left for Vietnam.
You've cut yourself out of it,
torn your half in pieces
and lain them on the mantle,
where your knickknacks used to be:
those godawful Hummels you'd been collecting for years
and a small glass vial you said
contained your grandmother's tears.
A thick film of dust comes off on my fingers,
when I rub them across the years
that came to separate us.

In a corner of the living room, facing a wall,
I find my last painting of you.
In it, you lie, naked, on the old iron bed,
your head hanging over the side,
your hair, flowing to the floor
like a wide, black river.
There, Max, the cat, is curled
in a gray, purring blur,
all fur and gooseberry green eyes that stare at me,

as if accusing me of some indiscretion
he doesn't dare mention.
Suddenly, he meows loudly
and rises as if he's been spooked,
runs through the house,
then swoops back to his place beside you,
and beside the night table,
on which I've painted a heart on a white plate,
and a knife and fork on a red-checkered napkin.
You hate the painting. You say I'm perverse
to paint you that way, and worse, an amateur.
"Do you want to tear out my heart and eat it
like the Aztecs used to do,
so you can prove you don't need me?" you ask.
"But I do need you," I say. "That's the point."
"I don't get it," you say,
as you dress for some party
you claim you are going to, but I'm on to your game.
It's your lover who's waiting for you.
"I know who he is," I say,
"but I don't know his name,"
then I run to the bathroom,
grab a handful of Trojans
and throw them at you,
as you slam the door on me,
before I can slam it on you.
You don't come back, until you get word
that I've enlisted in the army.
I'm packing, when you show up.
"You heard," I say
and you tell me that it's perverse of me too.

"Who are you kidding, you, a soldier?
And what's that?" you ask.
I give you the small canvas I've just finished.
"A sample of my new work," I say.
"There's nothing on it," you say.
"That's right," I tell you. "It's white like the plate,
after I ate your heart."
"Don't start," you say, "don't."
We part with a brief kiss like two strangers
who miss the act of pressing one mouth
against another, yet resist, resist.
We part on a day just like this,
a day that seems as if it will never end,
in an explosion that sends my body
flying through the air
in the white glare of morning,
when without warning, I step on a land mine
and regain consciousness to find
I'm a notation on a doctor's chart that says,
BK amputee.

Now I imagine myself racing through the house
just as Max did once,
only to return to myself, to the bed,
the night table, the canvas in my lap
and my brush, poised above it.
When Max, toothless and so old,
his hair comes out in clumps, when I touch him,
half sits, half collapses beside my wheelchair,
I begin to paint, first a black background,
then starting from the left side,

a white line, beside a red line,
beside a white, beside a red,
each one getting smaller and smaller,
until they disappear off the edge of the canvas.
I title it *Amateur.*
I call it art.

FLASHBACK

For Norman Fox

I'm on my way to work
at the Tackn' Feed shop
of which I own fifty-five percent,
when I hear sirens behind me
and pull over as three cop cars,
an ambulance, unmarked van, and a firetruck zoom past.
Not two minutes later, I start to sweat.
My heart beats rapidly
and I get that old feeling of dislocation
as my truck rocks like a cradle.
I grip the steering wheel the way I always do
when the pit bulls of bad memory
threaten to chew off my hands.
I count to twenty and drive on,
but as I pass the abortion clinic,
suddenly, I am in country again,
snorting pure heroin.
It's setting off flares in my brain,
tracers and those psychedelic snakes
I hallucinate are crawling all over me,
until I jump out of the truck,
which somehow I have driven onto the sidewalk.
I am using the open door for cover,
when Captain Kiss My Ass yells,
"Get down there where Charlie's holed up."
Waste the motherfucker. Motherfucker, I think.
I hear Simpson screaming something

and I am screaming too
and running through the elephant grass and bullets.
Someone steps on a land mine,
but it's nothing to me.
I am focused on my objective,
which is to wipe out the enemy,
but who is he?
"Bud, Bud, you OK?" I hear a voice call.
It's Harley, the guy who works at 7-Eleven.
He says, "Right to Lifers
threatened to blow up the clinic again."
I don't want to know anything about it,
even though I have a personal connection to the place.
"Need some help?" he asks.
"No thanks, man, I'm OK," I tell him, but I am shaking,
as if I am still trying to kick back in Saigon.
My girlfriend squeezes tepid water on my face
from a dirty towel and clucks her tongue,
as if I'm the one who needs sympathy.
"Save it," I tell her, shoving her hand away.
I don't need anything but a way out.
I had it for a while,
but I could not give myself over to the drug.
Even when I was high, I always felt
as if I were up above my body watching myself
pretend to descend into my own hell,
which even the Devil had abandoned
for more fertile ground.
My hell was just a hole in the ground
at the bottom of which the captain waited.
I hated him, but in an almost loving way,
for like a bad parent, he made me what I was

and what I am, despite my settled life,
my wife, kids, a savings account,
and once-a-year vacations to Barbados.
So many men died, because of his ambition.
He'd send us into more dangerous situations
than he had to, so he could make himself
a hotshot with the yahoos,
back at headquarters.
He had one eye on the slaughter
and one fixed on war's end,
when he'd use its career boost
and ascend the ladder of of command.
I was just a grunt, humping my ass,
but I could shoot even better than I could breathe.
He needed me, so most times he left me alone
and focused on some other slob,
Simpson, another old-timer and volunteer like me,
Miller, Dean, Johnson, Macafee, Sanchez, or Willoughby,
our latest "FNG." We didn't use his name at first,
but called him Fucking New Guy,
until I said I'd "marry" him
and teach him the ropes.
I'd been in country twice and in the bush
more times than I cared to think about.
I can admit now that I liked war,
but I didn't like killing the way Miller did,
or that kid who fell on sharpened bamboo poles
hidden in a foliage-covered hole.
One even went through his asshole and ruptured his guts,
which spilled all over the ground,
when we pulled him off the poles.
"Like a stuck pig," said Johnson,

as he sat back on his heels,
looking down at the bloodstained bamboo.
Then he used a flamethrower to incinerate them.
"Anybody for barbecue?" he asked.
That set off a round of jokes about the Fourth of July
and by the time we got back to base camp,
we were good and hungry.
The CO didn't join in. He never did.
He hid behind his mirrored sunglasses and his commands.
He could give you a death sentence
with a smile and a handshake.
He'd say, "Men, make me proud"
and if we didn't, next time he sent us on patrol,
we knew he'd have us taking fire no matter how intense,
not caring whether we all went home in body bags,
as long as he survived to receive his medals
from the boardroom generals and jive-ass politicians
who only played at war.

Finally, I get back in my truck,
as the unneeded bomb squad, cops, and firemen start to leave.
I should too, but I just sit
only half aware of my surroundings
and watch as a protester is lead to a police car.
I see it is my wife, Pam,
who must have violated the court order
to stay one hundred feet
from the entrance of the clinic again.
She notices me and waves,
just as a cop pushes her into the backseat,
but I imagine I see Captain Kiss,
waving me on toward the lair of the VC

who wasted Macafee and Simpson,
who had just become a short-timer.
Since I am the only old salt left,
the others look to me for some semblance of reason,
but they also realize I'm itching for a confrontation
and the captain has given me permission
to make the VC pay for every shitty day
I've been in my self-made exile.
When Sanchez says, "Waste the sonofabitch"
and Captain Kiss for once is outrunning me,
firing like he really means it,
until maybe he realizes what he is doing
and slows and seeks cover,
I can't resist screaming "Yellow dog" at him,
but he doesn't hear me as I run past,
zeroing in on the hole, where the tunnel rat
is dug in with a machine gun
and God knows it's booby-trapped,
so even if he dies, he'll take more of us with him.
Suddenly, I slow down, until I come to a full stop.
I'm hit, I think, almost relieved
as I sink to the ground.
I'm ready to die. I want to die,
having at last found the peace
that only comes when you cease to struggle
against the inevitable
and intense disintegration of body and soul,
but my survival instinct takes hold
and I manage to get up on my knees
and see the captain as he retreats
even farther from the fray.
I can't get to my launcher,

so I throw the grenade as far as I can
and remember only the terrific force as it explodes,
but soundless and somehow divorced from time,
while I am outside myself,
just swimming in the amniotic sack of destiny.
When I finally drag myself to where I last saw the captain,
there's nothing left but dog tags splashed with blood
and a few shreds of cloth.
I want to cry, but I don't.
I just lie on my back, listening to the eerie quiet
as the bloodshot-eyed afternoon stumbles off
and early evening arrives with the fanfare of rats
scurrying through the grass.
I remember the sapper who attacked the transit facility
the night I arrived in Vietnam.
She wasted four men, when she detonated her grenades.
I wonder why she chose certain death,
when she could have thrown them and perhaps survived?
Should I have done the same? I wonder,
as I hear someone coming toward me.
It's the VC.
I wait for him to take me out,
but he only bends closer and closer,
then he smiles and says, "I see you,"
and raises his arm, pretending to throw.
Then he stabs me with my own K-bar.
The rest is insignificant, is just evac and recovery,
is going through the motions back in the world.
Now I use my family like a magic potion
to get me through the memories
that are more real than the life I lead,
but nothing really eases my conscience.

Sometimes I even pretend the captain
has come home at last
with the ugly past forgotten
and the present rotten with happiness.
Maybe he's a general now too,
or a senator who won't give a guy like me the time of day.
Ain't that the way? I think,
as I choke on the stink of the last twenty-eight years
and have to light a cigarette
and suck it really hard.
I start the truck and head downtown,
where I will bail Pam out of jail
and never tell her about the crime I committed,
which at the time seemed necessary,
seemed like the very essence of the meaning
of the word, *soldier.*

MOMENTO MORI

for Jim & Turner Davis, artists

Twenty years ago, you were the man
who tended my roses, Jim,
but that ended in the garden of friendship,
where nothing grows
so much as serves its time,
frozen in the poses of love.
Those scissors you wielded like a surgeon
cut away that version of me
and now you don't know who I am
beneath my clothes.
My body's changed.
It's grown older
and rearranged itself to suit
some other truth, or lie.
I said good-bye. I meant it,
until I met you
stumbling through the rye again.
I could have let you pass,
but I caught a reflection of you
in a shot glass
and when I raised my eyes
your son was standing there to my surprise.
Now he's the one whose touch
I dream sends me reeling
from desk and chair, to bed
to rest my face on the pillow
where he lays his head,

where I take him on my tongue
like a sacrament,
where I am the paint he strokes on the canvas,
until the image he creates is my face
transfigured by desire,
my body surrounded by flames
and pierced by a single arrow.
I'll die for art, but not for love
and I sense he'll give me what I want,
still I choose to rendezvous
only in sleep,
until he crosses over the boundary of the unconscious
when one day, I run into him
at the Lucian Freud show (how fitting, no?).
Afterward, we go out for drinks.
He thinks he's so daring
when he says, "Damnit, let's go to bed,"
or something more romantic (I forget)
and we do,
though I mostly find lust a bore now.
I'd just as soon mop the floor as make love.
He understands. He knows I go
from one passion to the next
without a fixed destination.
He knows my inclination is to do
my loving with my mind and not my body.
I don't use men. I lose them
in the rough seas of my imagination,
where aroused and afraid,
they give in to my domination,
before they disappear.
Cleverly, he plays the role

of slave so skillfully,
I decide to free him,
but he says, "Beat me, use your fists."
I use a whip instead.
When I draw blood, I stop,
but he begs me to go on
and I do, until my strength is gone
and we lie gasping in the long shadow
of night among the starving,
where you find us, Jim.
At first, you stare at us
as if we were merely objects,
then take up the brush
and paint us
as if we'd died this side of Paradise.

VISITATION

"Heaven and earth.
What else is there?"
Said Walt Whitman in your dream,
then he smiled at you
and disappeared,
but you wanted him to come back.
You wanted to tell him that there was more.
There was the hardsell
you had to give yourself to stay alive
HIV positive five years
and counting backward to the day
your other life was stripped
bare of its leaves
at the start of the war of disease
against the body.
You don't have AIDS,
yet, you know it's coming
like a train whose whistle
you can hear before you see it.
When you feel the tremors
of internal earthquake,
will you do the diva thing?
Will you Rudolf Nureyev your way on stage,
so ravaged and dazed
you don't know who you are,
or commit your public suicide in private,
windows open wide

on the other side,
where your father, Walt is waiting
to take you in his arms
like a baby returning there on waking,
beside the picnic basket
in the long grass,
where the brittle pages of a book
are turning to the end.

STAR VEHICLE (MY SENIOR YEAR IN HIGH SCHOOL)

One loud whistle, then another
blots out the sound of Mother's screams,
as she runs alongside the railroad tracks,
where my best friend Suzy and I sit,
our backs to the oncoming train.
I didn't plan on Mother finding out.
I thought I could just die in peace,
without her interfering,
but she must have read my journal,
which she promised she would never do.
Looking back, I should have known.
Mother is parent to the bone
and not the older sister she wants to be.
She wants control.
The day I told her I wouldn't go to her alma mater,
she told me how much I'd disappointed her.
I was fed up and so was Suzy,
whose father had grounded her for smoking cigarettes!!
Suzy told him she wanted to die cool.
Anyway, we were sick of bullshit rules
that make a girl go crazy.
I don't know why we didn't just drink rat poison,
or hire Jimmy Barnes to do it.
He said he would for the thrill
of killing stupid bitches,
but I abhor boys who condescend to me.

I had high scores on my SATs.
I told him I didn't need his help.
I'd think of something
and he yelled in front of everyone
in the cafeteria
that Suzy and I were cunts,
then Robby, my old boyfriend punched him
and got suspended for two weeks
and that day ended
and another one began just like the other,
but as I was watching VH-1
and RuPaul was showing us all how to be a woman
just like a man,
it came to me that we needed to do something dramatic.
We had to be drama queens
and snap our fingers at the world and mean it.
I told Suzy what we would do
and she was even more into it than I was.
She *wanted* to commit suicide.
She even planned her outfit down to her Calvin Klein thong.
I told her it didn't matter what we wore.
I was already feeling kind of weird about it,
but we'd sworn an oath of sisterhood
and pricked ourselves with pins
we'd dipped in alcohol to kill the germs,
so I couldn't back out. Not then anyway.
I promised myself that I would stop it,
before it was too late,
but before I knew it, I was holding her hand,
as the freight train from hell (downtown L.A.),
rolled down the tracks.
When I tried to let go of Suzy's hand,

she held on tighter
and I couldn't get free,
but as I prepared myself for death
by imagining Brad Pitt would save me,
I got the strength to save myself.
I balled my free hand in a fist
and hit Suzy in the face.
She released my hand
and I got up and ran across the tracks
to my mother, who had fainted,
the way she always does when things don't go her way.
That's when I changed my mind
about the whole thing
and screamed, "Suzy, I'm coming back,"
but just then, the train splattered Suzy
all over the tracks.
I sat beside my mother, rocking back and forth
like a crazy person, or a drug addict,
until the cops and ambulance arrived.
I survived, because I have a well-developed
sense of self-preservation,
at least that's what my shrink says.
Mother told the cops I tried to save Suzy
and nearly got killed myself.
She told them I was a hero.
"Heroine, Mom," I said.
A few days later, I scanned Dad's morning newspaper,
as I dipped my biscotti in my latte,
but Suzy and I were already old news.
Later, I went to Neiman's
and bought a pair of high heel velvet mules
with pointed toes

that made my legs look great,
when I danced for the first time in ages
at the rave held in Suzy's honor.
I was so glad to be alive,
I didn't even need X
and when the hunk with the shaved head came up to me,
I grabbed his balls.
He went down on me later, in the bathroom
at Einstein's Bagels.
They asked us to leave.
I got mad and threw my lox at the waitress
and we ran and ran, until I remembered I'd left my car
in the parking lot.
I got Robby to go back for it
and we smoked some grass behind his dad's house
and made love for old times' sake,
then I made him take me to a strip club,
where I stripped down to my thong.
It was a long night.
Then I felt so sad I knew I was in mourning
and I had him take me home.
Mother and Dad were out of town for the weekend
and I went in their room.
When I looked in the nightstand drawer,
I found vaginal lubricant, condoms and handcuffs!!
I knew I'd had enough. I needed a vacation,
so I crammed some clothes in my backpack
and got to LAX in time to catch a plane to Tahiti,
where I sat on the beach,
letting the sun, not Clairol, bleach my hair
and pretended I was exactly where I wanted to be,
until I was so bored

I booked passage on a freighter.
I had dinner with the captain,
strolled the deck with Mabel,
an Englishwoman and her Maltese, Ralph,
pronounced Rafe
and fucked the first mate
on top of a table in the dining room,
where they served roast beef, duck l'orange
and chicken Marengo
the night before we docked back in L.A.
It was good to be home after three long months
and I was even able to graduate.
I enrolled at USC film school
and had Suzy tattooed on my thigh,
so I wouldn't forget my best friend,
who was able to escape her fate, or maybe found it,
while I live my life surrounded by new friends.
Sometimes I still think life sucks,
but it's better than the alternative,
which never ends.
Thank God a movie does.

PASSING THROUGH

"Earth is the birth of the blues," sang Yellow Bertha,
as she chopped cotton beside Mama Rose.
It was as hot as any other summer day,
when she decided to run away.
Folks say she made a fortune
running a whorehouse in New Orleans,
but others say she's buried somewhere out west,
her grave unmarked,
though you can find it in the dark
by the scent of jasmine and mint,
but I'm getting ahead of myself.
If it wasn't for hell,
we'd all be tapdancing with the devil
Mama Rose used to say,
but as it is, we just stand and watch,
while someone else burns up before salvation.
"People desire damnation, Bertha," she said,
unwrapping the rag from her head
to let the sweat flow down the corn rows,
plaited as tightly as the night coming down
on the high and mighty on judgment day.
They say she knew what was coming,
because she threw some bones that morning.
She bent down to pick up her rag which had fallen
and when she straightened up, her yellow gal
had gone down the road.
"Go then," she called out, "I didn't want you no how."

Then she started talking to herself
about how Old White John caught her milking cows.
"He wrestled me to the ground and did his nastiness."
He said, "your daddy was a slave and his daddy
and I'm claiming back what's mine."
It was July. I remember fireworks going off outside.
When Bertha come, so white
she liked to scared me to death,
I let her suckle my breast
and I said, "All right, little baby,
maybe I'll love you. Maybe."
Mama Rose said she did her best,
but it's hard to raise a gal like that
with everybody thinking she's giving them the high hat,
because she's so light and got those green eyes
that look right through you. She frightens people.
Even men, who're usually wanting to saddle up
and ride that kind of mare, can't abide her.
They're afraid if they try her, they'll never be the same.
The only ones willing are white.
They're watching her day and night,
but they know John swore to kill any man
who touched her,
because lo and behold, he owns up to her.
He's proud of her. Nobody can believe it.
He's even at her baptism.
He buys her cheap dresses and candy at the store.
He hands it to her out the door,
because she can't go in.
He won't, he won't stop looking at her
like it's some kind of miracle she was born
looking so much like him and his people.

It's a warning, or something.
"It's evil turning back on itself," said the preacher
the Sunday cut clean through by the truth,
by the living proof, as Old John stood up in church
and testified to the power of God,
who spoke to him that morning,
telling him he was a sinner.
He died that winter. Horrible suffering, they say.
He had a stroke on the way to town.
His car ran off the road and he drowned.
They say Bertha found him.
They say she ran all the way to town for the doctor,
who told her, "I am not a colored doctor,"
so she went and got the sheriff.
He listened for a while, then he locked her in a cell.
He said he knew she was guilty of something.
Well, after a while, Rose went down there
and I swear she nearly had a fit.
"Get my daughter out here," she said.
"How can you lock up your own brother's child?"
The sheriff knew it was true, so finally he said,
"You take her and don't ever cross my path again."
When Bertha passed him on the way out,
he tripped her with his foot.
When she got off the floor, she said,
"Every dog has its day."

From that time to this is a straight line,
pointing at a girl,
who doesn't even have shoes anymore,
as she runs down the road,
throwing off her ragged clothes, as she goes,

until she's as naked as the day she was born.
When she comes to washing hanging on the line,
she grabs a fine dress and keeps on running.
She's crying and laughing at the same time.
Along comes a truck that says J. GOODY on the side.
The man driving stops to give her a ride.
He swings the door open on the passenger side,
but Bertha says, "Move over, I'll drive."
When she asks him why he stopped,
he says, "I know white trash, when I see it.
You're just like me, but you're a girl. You're pretty.
You can free yourself. All you have to do
is show a little leg and some titty in the big city."
He gave her fifty cents and a wink
and she started thinking she might as well turn white.
She got a job waiting table in a dance hall.
One night, the boss heard her
singing along with the band.
He said, "Why don't you go up on stage,"
and she said, "I play piano too."
He said, "Howdy do."
From then on, she made everybody pay
one way, or another.
She got hard. She took lovers—
fathers, sons, and husbands.
It didn't matter,
but once in a while, she heard her mother's voice,
saying, "You made the wrong choice,"
and she felt the blues
and she let loose with a shout.
"Lordy," said the boss, "you sound colored."
More and more people came to hear her sing,

but they kind of feared her too.
They said, she was too white to sing the blues like that.
It wasn't right.
One night, she got to talking with the boss.
He walked round and round the office, shaking his head,
saying how much he'd lose,
if she stopped singing the blues.
"How often can you find a treasure like mine," he said,
laying his hand on her shoulder,
then he said, "If I weren't so old,"
and his voice dropped off to a whisper,
then he said, "I got the answer now, sweet Roberta.
Go on down to the dressing room and wait."
It didn't take long.
He came in and set a jar on the table.
"What do I do with this?" Asked Bertha.
He said, "you're going to pass for colored."
Suddenly, she was wearing blackface.
Suddenly, she was safe on the other side
of the door she slammed on the past
and it was standing open at last.
She could come and go as she pleased
and no one saw her enter, or leave.
She was free, she was freed,
but she didn't feel it
and she needed it to be real.
She went on, though. She flowed like a river,
carrying the body of a man,
who had himself a nigger, because he could.
She lived. She got old.
She almost froze one cold spell
and she got up from her sickbed

and told her daughter
she got during the change of life
it was time to go.
She sewed a note to her ragged coat.
It said, *"This is the granddaughter of Mama Rose."*
She put fifty cents in her hand
and went to stand with her at the bus stop.
She would not return, but her child
had earned the right to go home.

When I got off the bus,
a hush fell over the people waiting there.
I was as white as my mother,
but my eyes were gray, not green.
I had hair down to my waist and braids so thick
they weighed me down.
Mother said, my father was a white musician
from another town,
who found out her secret
and left her and me to keep it.
Mama Rose knew me, though, blind as she was.
"What color are you, gal?" She asked
and I told her, "I'm as black as last night."
That's how I passed, without asking permission.

INDEX